Civilizing the Internet

Civilizing the Internet

Global Concerns and Efforts Toward Regulation

Joseph Migga Kizza

McFarland & Company, Inc., Publishers
Jefferson, North Carolina, and London

British Library Cataloguing-in-Publication data are available

Library of Congress Cataloguing-in-Publication Data

Kizza, Joseph Migga.
    Civilizing the internet : global concerns and efforts toward
regulation / by Joseph Migga Kizza.
        p.   cm.
    Includes index.
    ISBN 0-7864-0539-2 (sewn softcover : 50# alkaline paper) ∞
    1. Internet (Computer network)—Social aspects.   2. Internet
(Computer network)—Government policy.   I. Title.
HM221.K588   1998
303.48'33—dc21   98-26316
                                                                CIP

Manufactured in the United States of America

*McFarland & Company, Inc., Publishers
    Box 611, Jefferson, North Carolina 28640*

To Immaculate, Josephine and Florence Kizza
for cherishing that which keeps us strong

Contents

Acknowledgments

I want to acknowledge here the considerable help I received in the form of ideas and criticisms from colleagues around the world. The criticisms were particularly helpful because on a number of occasions they forced me to reexamine my line of argument. I want to pay a particular tribute to my dear wife, Dr. Immaculate Kizza, not because of her unending love, which I unfortunately take for granted, but because of the long hours she put into this project. I am also very grateful to Dr. Victoria Steinberg of the University of Tennessee, Chattanooga, for her excellent translation of the French Internet Charter.

A book with a global scope like this one cannot be done without a considerable amount of input from colleagues with expertise in their fields. I want to thank the following colleagues for their timely input: Diane Whitehouse from the U.K., who right from the start showed great interest in the project and suggested many valuable sources of material; Jacques Berleur of the University of Nemur, Belgium; John Weckert of Charles Sturt University, Australia; Margo Langford, Corporate and Regulatory Counsel, in Canada; and Nicholas Ros de Lochounoff of Transiceil, France.

I am also grateful to the following people and companies for granting me permission to reproduce certain items: Stephen Balkam, Executive Director of RSAC; Wendy Simpson, President of SafeSurf; David Weskey of Information Resources and Communications, President's Office,

University of California for the use of the Internet2 concept; and Sun Microsystems Software.

Finally, I want to pay tribute to all those people who in one way or another helped in any form but whose names I have not included here.

Joseph Migga Kizza

Preface

From its humble beginning as a research project in the 1960s, the Internet has grown into a dominant global infrastructure of networked computers supporting millions of users in over 160 countries. It is believed that this network will grow to billions of nodes within the next decade, connecting nearly every human being on earth.

The Internet has resurrected the romantic myth of boundless space beyond the frontiers of known human civilization. New frontiers abound with infinite opportunities, where individuals can easily shed birth identities to acquire any identity of choice and where laws are self-made and observed (or broken) at will.

Caught by the spell of this myth, thousands of earthlings have logged on to the Internet, causing a massive and extremely rapid growth of this new medium. Besides creating a virtual landscape approaching utopia, the Internet has also created problems in the governance of real societies by subverting accepted norms, laws, and values. The most affected domains are telecommunications, broadcasting and computer services. Different nations have regulated those three domains distinctly and with varying degrees depending on national priorities. For example in Canada broadcasting is more regulated than telecommunications, whereas in the United States the field of telecommunications seems to be more regulated than broadcasting.

In every country the laws governing these different domains have been distinct until now. With the advent of the Internet, there has been a convergence of these three media. The Internet has fostered this convergence, resulting in a medium encompassing all the attributes of telecommunications, broadcasting and computer services. This convergence has resulted in confusion because policies and definitions that used to be precise are no longer. Such confusion has created muddles, frustrations, problems and, for some, opportunities in the interpretation and implementation of policies in the Internet medium. The Internet medium consequently has given a new exposure to all sorts of human vices, giving them a new arena and, to some extent, a veiled degree of legitimacy. Such deeds have caught many civic groups, communities, regional groupings and governments off-guard, and many are struggling to come up with guidelines, policies and in some cases censorship mechanisms to regulate the Internet, which they see as getting out of control.

This book discusses the convergence of the three media by looking at the *whole* Internet through its historical development, its globalization, the concerns it has brought, the tools available to deal with these concerns on a variety of levels, and the efforts being undertaken by regional groupings and national governments around the globe to regulate the medium. To highlight the seriousness of the problems, the level of global concern, and the efforts being undertaken to meet the Internet challenge, the author has spent a considerable amount of time on three chapters: chapter three, dealing with the complex nature of Internet concerns; chapter four, examining a variety of tools at the disposal of every Internet user; and chapter five, detailing the ongoing global efforts at regulation.

The book is not intended as a survey or an endorsement of any working policies and charters, but as an analysis and discussion of attempts being made around the globe to regulate the Internet. It is meant to show that although not much can be done in controlling the Internet without serious violation of individual rights, efforts are being made by communities and governments around the world to make the Internet an effective communications infrastructure for the twenty-first century and beyond. As Kevin Werbach, the Federal Communications Commission consul for new technology policy, puts it, "Improvements in communications technology will continue to provide myriad benefits for individuals, businesses and society. ... In the long run, the endless spiral of connectivity is more powerful than any government edict."*

*Kevin Werbach. "Digital Tornado: The Internet and Telecommunications Policy." FCC Staff Working Paper on Internet Policy, March 27, 1997.

The book targets college students in information technology studies and engineering and, to a lesser extent, students in the arts and sciences who are interested in information technology. But students in computer and engineering sciences, computer information sciences and management, and library sciences will find the book particularly helpful. And practitioners, especially those working in information-intensive areas such as insurance and banking, will also find the book a good reference source. It will also be valuable to those interested in any aspect of the Internet and to those simply wanting to become Internet literate.

Chapter 1

The Structure and Development of the Internet

Historical Development

The Internet, a global network of computers, originated from the early work of J. C. R. Licklider of MIT on "Galactic Networks." Licklider conceptualized global interconnected sets of communication channels, programs and data sites which could be accessed quickly from any site (1). The networking concept envisioned by Licklider would support communication among network nodes using a concept of packets instead of circuits, thus enabling computers to talk to each other.

Although the MIT work created the momentum for the packet-switching network concept, it was not the only work on the concept. There were two additional independent projects on this same topic: that of Donald Davies and Roger Scantleberg at the British National Laboratory (BNL), which later was credited with coining the term "packet," and that of Paul Baran at RAND (1). The computer network concept was tested in 1965 when Thomas M. Roberts used a low-speed dial-up telephone line to connect the TX-2 computer at Boston on the East coast of the United States to the Q-32 computer in Los Angeles on the West coast, creating the first working Wide Area Network (WAN). This experiment opened the door for all computer network communications we use today.

Although the scientists of that time provided the concept, the technical know-how and the personnel to build the beginnings of the Internet, the financial component and support of the concept came from politicians and military planners with cold war concerns about the survival of U.S. communication in the aftermath of a nuclear attack.

In a paper titled "Packet Switching Networks for Secure Voice," written in 1964, the think tank at Rand Corporation proposed the computer network concept, which had thus far been in the academic arena, to the military. The paper proposed a network structure that has (a) no central authority so that all nodes in the network are equal in status, each capable of originating, passing on and receiving messages from any other and (b) an infrastructure of bits and pieces working in unison. To facilitate this infrastructure, messages were to be divided into independently and individually addressed "packets" that would flow from source node to destination node through possibly one or more intermediary nodes. Such a network structure fitted the military and administrative thinking that if one piece of the network were disabled, others would function as if the network were still whole (1).

With the U.S. Department of Defense underwriting the project, the concept was put in motion with coordinated research activities at Rand, Massachusetts Institute of Technology (MIT), University of California Los Angeles (UCLA), and the British National Physical Laboratory (NPL). The first working models of the network were tested at MIT, UCLA and NPL by the late 1960s. U.S. efforts resulted in the first network installation code, named ARPANET, at UCLA in 1969(2). The selection of UCLA to host the first Interface Message Processor (IMP) to support the first node of ARPANET was in recognition of Licklider's outstanding early work in the development of the packet-switching theory. The second node was installed at Stanford to support Doug Englebart's work on "Augmentation of Human Intellect," and shortly after, others were installed at UC Santa Barbara and at the University of Utah (1). In subsequent years the number of nodes on ARPANET increased as more research institutions and universities got connected, and by 1970 there were 37 nodes in the United States (2). Because the network was primarily in the hands of researchers and the academic elite, these people were able to access these federally funded remote and dear computer resources to collaborate and share research notes on their projects. The general public got its first glimpse of this new technology in 1972 at the International Computer Communication Conference (ICCC) and this was also the year when e-mail, which came to be the main mover of the Internet, was introduced.

As the number of nodes increased, more universities joined the exclusive club, and ARPANET became not only a research facilitator but a free federally funded postal system of electronic mail. In 1984 the U.S. National Science Foundation (NSF) joined ARPANET in starting its own network code named NSFNET. NSFNET set a new pace in nodes, bandwidth, speed and upgrades. This NSF-funded network brought the Internet within reach for many universities throughout the United States and the world that could not otherwise afford the costs, and many government agencies also joined in. At this point other countries and regions were establishing their own networks.

With so much success and fanfare, ARPANET ceased to exist in 1989. As the number of nodes on the Internet climbed into hundreds of thousands worldwide, the role of sponsoring agencies like ARPA and NSF became more and more marginalized. Eventually in 1994 NSF also ceased its support of the Internet. The Internet by now needed no helping hand because it had assumed a momentum of its own.

Organization of the Internet

As I pointed out in the last section, the Internet is a decentralized network of computers with no one node having higher status than any other node. Yet the Internet is reliable, at least to some, and is the most sophisticated electronic network ever built. Decentralization and synchronization rarely go together, yet the Internet, which combines both of these design philosophies, is as efficient a communication network as it is sophisticated. The question then is whether there is something underlying the structure and organization of the Internet that we do not know? There is. In fact, the Internet is organized around not one but four core themes. These themes are topology, communication media, bandwidth and management. We will now look at each of these themes in more detail.

Topology

The Internet is a meganetwork comprising multiple independent networks of arbitrary designs including packet satellite networks and ground-based package radio networks (see Figure 1.1). For all these net-works to work efficiently and in unison, there must be an underlying technical philosophy. For the Internet this philosophy is called "open archi-tecture," meaning that any individual member network technology in the Internet combo is not dictated by any particular architecture but is selected freely by a provider. Individual networks may have different designs and development, and each may have its own unique interface based on envi-ronment and user requirements.

The open architecture idea was introduced by Kahn, and according to Barry Leiner et al. (1), the networks would observe the following ground rules:

1. Each distinct network would have to stand on its own, and no inter-nal changes would be required for any such network to connect to the Internet.
2. Communication would be on the best-effort basis; that is, if a packed transmission is not successful, it would be retransmitted.
3. Black boxes would be used to connect to networks.
4. There would be no local control at any operation level.

Kahn's black boxes are now called gateways and routers. These routers connect the network to a high-speed circuit that transmits data based on a specific protocol so that there is synchronization of transmission activi-ties with all other routers in the meganetwork. The most popular Inter-net networks are the Local Area Network (LAN) and the Wide Area Net-work (WAN).

Local Area Network (LAN)

A LAN is a network of computers covering a small area like a floor in a building or a university campus. LAN technologies include Ethernet, Token Ring, Fast Ethernet, FDDI, and 100VG-AnyLAN. Each has its advantages and disadvantages over the others, but they are all good for pro-viding high-speed connectivity within the defined areas of the network. LANs can be either peer to peer, a very small network consisting of a few computers, or client to server, usually bigger networks like those serving large corporations. LANs are built mostly using two topologies: star and bus. A star topology involves a central hub computer to which all other computers are connected. Intercommunication between computers must be channeled through this hub computer. In a bus topology all comput-ers are individually connected to the transmission medium and intercom-

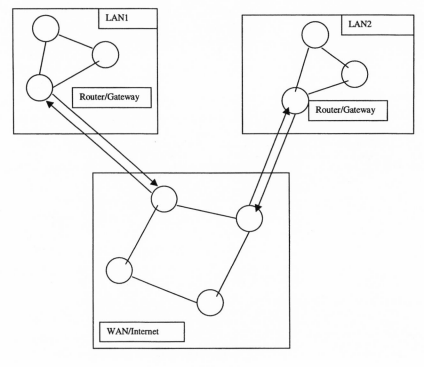

Figure 1.1

munication is carried through each individual computer. These two topologies handle system failures differently. For example in a star topology if any computer other than the hub fails, the system continues to function. However in a bus topology, if one intermediate computer collapses, the whole system is brought down. See Figure 1.2.

Data Transmission in a LAN. Data frames or packets sent across a LAN network reach all attached computers in the network. How then can two computers communicate when all computers in the network receive the same frame? Each computer on the network has a unique physical address represented by a number. So a frame sent across a LAN contains the addresses of the source and destination computers. Each computer receives the frame and compares its address and the recipient address on the frame. Upon recognizing its address on the frame, the recipient computer accepts the frame and can also send acknowledgment using the sender address. Many LAN and WAN technologies use these broadcast techniques.

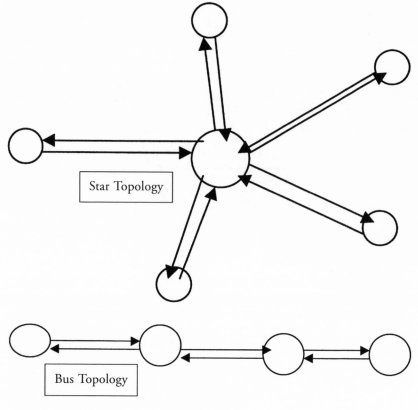

Figure 1.2

Wide Area Networks (WAN)

A WAN is a network that connects many computers and covers a large area. Many times a WAN allows interconnections between LANs across town or across the country.

Packet Switching in a WAN. Networks contain electronic devices that cause the hardware to connect to one or more computers, allowing them to transfer data selectively. A switch is like a multiport hub, with each port attached to a computer. Because a packet switch is the basic building block of a WAN, WANs can keep all computers on the network communicating through a store-and-forward technique in which packets arriving at a switch are placed in a queue waiting for their destinations to be switched on.

Packet Transmission in a WAN. Each computer in a WAN is assigned a physical address. When a computer in a WAN is sending a frame to another computer in a WAN, the sending computer must supply the recipient computer's address just like in a LAN. Many WANs use a hierarchy addressing scheme that divides the address into logical parts, usually two. The first part identifies a packet switch, and the second part identifies the receiving computer attached to the packet switch.

WAN Technologies. WANs come in different technologies, each with its own advantages, but for our discussion we will focus only on the following:

1. Integrated Services Digital Network (ISDN). This technology uses twisted-pair telephone lines to transmit voice, data and graphics simultaneously. It transmits data in two modes: basic and primary rate. In a basic rate the most commonly used connections are low-rate bandwidth connections — like in small office, home office and remote communications — using either two simultaneous 64kps B-channels or a 16kps D-channel. In a primary rate, however, the network uses a higher-bandwidth interface of about 128kps or higher to combine basic connections. ISDN is very secure and fast, and it has high-quality connections because it offers an end-to-end digital connection. But primary ISDN is not very popular because of its costs.

2. Packet Switching. This involves the transmission of data as packets routed between the source and destination computers via a variety of routes to avoid system overloads. Unlike links in the ISDN, the path established is temporary and random and can be shared by other packets. There are two types of packet switching:
   - Frame Relay, which supports transmissions of variable-length packets across the network.
   - Asynchronous Transfer Mode (ATM), which is used in fixed-length packet transmission.

   Among the many advantages of packet switching are the following:

   Many different users can use the same telecommunications lines at the same time instead of a line being used by only one person at a time.

   Packets are passed from computer host to computer host until they reach their destination, creating many possible routes so that if a particular route is overloaded or disrupted, an alternate route is used.

   When errors occur, only affected packets need be retransmitted.

3. X.25: This is a packet transmission protocol that works by defining procedures for exchanging data between a user device and a network node. The X.25 came about to fill a need for interconnecting independent networks. It is therefore a common interface protocol. The connection established between the user station and the network node switches is usually done via a leased line. Transmission calls for an establishment of a connection before data can be transmitted. Sometimes acknowledgment is requested from both sides, and packets are transmitted in order. X.25 requires identification between the two communicating parties before full connection and transmission can start. Because of this it provides good security. But because of its ASCII terminal technology, this technology has become less and less popular and of course more expensive in today's digital communication marketplace (3).

Communication Medium

The computer network communication medium, which formed the basis for the TCP/IP protocol, was envisioned by Kahn and Cerf and was based on the following principles (1):

1. Communication between two processes consists of long streams of bytes called octets (which later came to be called packets).
2. Flow control is done using a sliding window and acknowledgment, where the destination selects when to acknowledge.
3. Source and destination nodes need to agree on parameters of the windowing used.

These ideas later formed the basis for the TCP/IP protocol. Following these principles, computer data, which is binary in both storage and transmission, is transferred between nodes in a network and between networks in small blocks of bits called packets. Packets are then sent individually and independently. Because of this computer networks are referred to as packet-switching networks or PSNs.

The motive behind packet switching is to divide the data to be transmitted from all source computers in the network into small packets so that no one computer can get exclusive or unfair advantage in the use of the transmission medium. This creates a situation in which all source computers have equal status in the network, and because packets are small, no computer experiences long delays in transmission. The details of the packet to be transmitted over the network are determined by the hardware technology of the network. Network hardware technology also determines the packaging of bits in packets.

Internet Bandwidth

The transmission lines between WANs and LANs are provided and maintained by big telecommunication companies commonly referred to as telcos. In the United States, these telcos include MCI, Sprint and World-comm. Below the telcos are the Internet Service Providers (ISPs). The ISPs lease circuit lines from the telcos. In the United States ISPs include America Online (AOL), MCI, UUnet, AGIS, Sprintnet, AT&T and many smaller companies. ISPs connect their routers in their respective points of presence (POP) to the leased lines, which connect to individual backbones scattered around their service areas. Different ISP backbones then have connections to the Network Access Points (NAPs), where they exchange traffic from their respective networks of backbones. The backbones usually receive fast feeds from the telcos, usually as high as 155Mbps depending on the country. The feeds are then sold to the ISP subscribers, usually at a very low speed, averaging 14.4Kbps depending on the modem speed.

Internet Management

Ever since founding organizations like ARPANET and NSF pulled out of underwriting the Internet, a number of cooperating organizations and groups have sprung up to provide the underlying organization and set basic policy for the Internet. The first-ever Internet coordinating bodies — the International Cooperation Board (ICB) and the Internet Configuration Control Board (ICCB), together with a European Internet Research Group dealing with Packet Satellites — were formed in the late 1970s to coordinate the activities of the expanding Internet. A few years later the Internet Activities Board was formed with different Task Forces, each focused on a different Internet technology. As the Internet's growth continued into the 1980s, new coordinating bodies emerged. The best-known of these loose organizations are the following:

The Internet Society (IS)

IS formed in 1992 and is an international nongovernmental organization of scientists and education professionals. IS aims to promote the evolution and use of the Internet and its technology on a worldwide basis, provide the organizational framework for the development of Internet Standards through the Internet Architecture Board and the Internet Engineering Task Force, and maintain and extend the availability and development of the Internet and its associated technologies to the global audience.

Internet Engineering Task Force (IETF)

IETF is another group formed in 1986 with a mandate to define new protocol engineering, development and application requirements for the Internet to serve a large open international community of network designers, operators, vendors and researchers who are concerned with the evolution of the Internet architecture and the smooth operation of the Internet.

Internet Architecture Board (IAB)

IAB is an advisory group of the Internet Society dealing with the technical aspects of the Internet standards for the global Internet and intranets and focusing more particularly, though not exclusively, on the TCP/IP protocol suite.

InterNIC

InterNIC is a loose group of several commercial organizations established in January of 1993 as a collaborative project between AT&T, General Atomics and Network Solutions, Inc. (NSI), and supported by the National Science Foundation. At its establishment InterNIC was to manage the InterNIC Directory and Database Services project while NSI managed the Registration Services project, and General Atomics the Information Services project. General Atomics was terminated in 1995, but two extra services were added. These were a) services provided by the Info Scout and b) second-level support to campus Network Information Center (NIC) organizations. The two services under NIC are now part of InterNIC known as InterNIC Information and Education Services and Net Scout Services. InterNIC, in addition, supports and participates in Internet forums, continues to support the Research and Education community to promote Internet services and explore new tools and technologies, and contributes to the rapidly growing Internet community (4).

Internet Protocol

The Internet is a network of hundreds of thousands of computers connected via modems to telephone communication lines or fiber-optic cables in both small and large networks. These computers communicate with each other in the network by utilizing a common set of technical protocols over a shared transmission medium. The sharing of the transmission medium by computers in this network inevitably petitions the network into clusters we earlier called LANs and even larger clusters we called WANs. Both LANs and WANs have become popular computer cluster networks on the Internet.

Although many computers connect to the Internet via networks, not all computers do. Many computers, especially those using modem dial-up connections, are not networked in any way. Such computers use temporary connections to connect to the Internet, usually via a dedicated gateway run by the Internet Service Provider (ISP). Even those in networks need not be permanently connected to each other but rather may have a temporary connection established for a duration with another computer in the network via what is commonly referred to as point-to-point configuration used in networks covering long distances.

But full Internet communication cannot be realized unless on top of this network infrastructure there is a working protocol supported by both hardware and software. The protocol customarily handles all low-level communications details over the network. Network software and hardware bring about a communication agreement that specifies the format and meaning of messages exchanged among the many different hardware and system software types of the computers and networks of the Internet.

This communication agreement functions as the protocol to bring about an intricate combination and collaboration of hundreds of differing network technologies to create a universal service with a seemingly common technology by hiding the details of physical network connections, addressing protocols and routing information. Different networks use different protocol suites, but the most common network protocols are the following:

Transmission Control Protocol/
Internet Protocol (TCP/IP)

TCP/IP is a leftover protocol suite from the ARPANET days composed of two protocols the Transmission Control Protocol (TCP) and the Internet Protocol (IP). The original version of TCP resulting from Kahn and Cerf's work not only supported packet switching between computer networks but also supported file transfer and remote login applications. However, in some areas of advanced network applications, especially in packet voice, packets got lost, and there was little chance that this could be corrected by TCP (1). This realization resulted in the formation of two protocols from the original TCP. These are:

1. Transmission Control Protocol (TCP): a part that transmits from computer to computer in the network. It is a reliable, connection-oriented, full-duplex stream transport level part of the TCP/IP suite that facilitates application programs on client computers to form connections, send data, receive data and terminate connections. TCP handles the service features of TCP/IP such as routing of packets, and in case the network becomes busy or unreliable, TCP tries to reroute the packets through other paths in the network. If a packet is not received by a preset time, or is erroneous, TCP requests a retransmission.

2. Internet Protocol (IP): the addressing and forwarding part of the TCP/IP suite. IP protocol defines an addressing scheme that assigns each computer connected on the Internet a unique address. Currently the IP addressing scheme uses a unique 32-bit binary number as an abstract address for each client. These addresses do not refer to physical computers but to the connections. But because very few users will ever remember a 32-bit string for an address, a dotted decimal notation is used. This scheme uses 8-bit sections (1 byte) as a decimal number. Each section is separated by a dot. But for convenience, dotted decimal addresses can be referred to by names commonly known as domain names. The domain name server scheme automatically converts the assigned DNS name to the 32-bit abstract address for the referenced computer. Besides assigning abstract addresses to each computer connected to the Internet, the IP scheme also assigns IP addresses to routers. Each router is initially assigned to one or more IP addresses because each router converts to multiple networks. For example, if a router connects to two networks, then it is assigned to two IP addresses.

Connecting to the Internet

There are basically two categories of Internet access: dial-up (sometimes referred to as terminal access) and direct connection.

Terminal access

Terminal, or dial-up, access is a slow and inconvenient service with a difficult interface that may sometimes not have all Internet services like file transfer protocol (FTP). It requires a pair of modems, one at each end of the communication line, and a telephone connection between the modems. Dial-up connections are overwhelmingly cheap. With a modem and corresponding software any computer can connect to the Internet. Modem connections are facilitated by local, national, and now increasingly international Internet Service Providers (ISP). To use an ISP's Internet service the user machine must have software that dials the ISP gateway, which then provides the client machine with TCP/IP protocol. The communication between the client machine and the ISP gateway is done via a modem and subsequent login. Once the connection is established between the two computers, the client computer appears as if it is directly connected to the Internet. The connected user may have been connected in one of the following ways:

1. Serial Line Internet Protocol (SLIP): uses a Serial Port connection.
2. Point-to-Point Protocol (PPP): a reliable IP protocol accessible via fast dial-up modems. The service stimulates your terminal, whatever the type, to look as an IP not directly connected to the Internet. To be able to successively get connected, the user must start the process through a sequence of commands. PPP then allows the user to use IPX, TCP/IP and Netberic protocol via a modem and over telephone lines.
3. UNIX-to-UNIX COPY (UUCP): a Unix software program protocol that allows Unix systems to exchange files including e-mail via serial links using modems at both ends of the serial link.
4. ON-LINE: involves one remote computer gaining access to a computer already connected to the Internet via terminal emulation communication software. This software, like the VT-100, allows a remote (usually home) computer to emulate a remote terminal attached to a host computer on the Internet.

Direct Connection

Direct connections have high-speed capabilities from 56 K bytes per second to 1.544 megabytes per second for a T-1 and 45 megabytes per second for a T-3 line connection. A T-1 line is usually a leased line carrying around 1.544 megabytes per second. Although this is the fastest technology available, so far, to carry data to the Internet, it is far below the 10 megabytes per second needed for a full screen and full motion video. A T-3 line is also a leased line, but this can carry 45 megabytes per second. T-3 communication is capable of full screen and full motion video communication. Direct connections also have better quality, move high data capacities and offer easy-to-use interfaces. The high speeds are made possible by new technologies like Asynchronous Transformer Mode (ATM), Synchronized Optical Networks (SON), and Integrated Services Digital Networks (ISDN).

These speeds and data capacities are, however, expensive. Direct connection requires expensive investment in equipment, scheduling, installation, maintenance and security. For example, before any connection is made a unique Internet protocol (IP address) must be acquired from the Internet Service Provider (ISP) or the InterNIC Registration Services Center, an IP registration service provider; the Operating System on the machine must be configured to run TCP/IP; a domain name must be established; serial network equipment like routers and digital modems must be in place; security must be in place to stop intruders, and maintenance and access costs must be agreed upon and budgeted for.

Internet Tools and Resources

The almost exponential growth of the Internet in the last few years indicates, if anything, that the Internet has a lot of goodies to offer. Such goodies are in the form of information and services. As the growth of the Internet has exploded, the appetite for information has skyrocketed, making it the most sought-after item on the Internet and cyclically making the Internet the primary source of this information. Now information has become the missing link, the vital part in almost every aspect of life and in all disciplines including education, health, industry, commerce and the list goes on and on. Thanks to the media, many have come to view the

Internet as the primary source of all types of information from news to how to make pumpkin pies.

Besides taking the Internet as the primary source of information, many are utilizing the speed of the Internet to move large quantities of data including personal and electronic mail, quickly, efficiently and cheaply. These features have made the Internet the de facto communication carrier and source of information for the next century.

Although the information on the Internet is plentiful and can be moved quickly, efficiently and cheaply, it is highly disorganized. So the process of searching for the right information, collecting it, and packaging it in the desired form is tedious and complex. Without the help of Internet tools such a task can only be done by a small fraction of people. However, the Internet offers several tools that can be used to locate, collect, organize and package information in any way we may desire. Among the most popular Internet tools are the following:

Communications

Electronic Mail (E-mail)

The e-mail system, consisting of different types of client software, was one of the maiden services of the Internet in its infancy; in fact, one can say that it has driven the growth of the Internet up to its present status because it enables the exchange of private communication between Internet users. Each user in the communication process is uniquely identifiable by an e-mail address, a two-part string of characters separated by the @ symbol as in the string: *User@server-name*. The first part of the string before the @ symbol uniquely identifies the user, and the second part after the @ symbol identifies the user's server. This part is a string of letters that may contain several stems separated by periods (.) like: *utcdc01.utc.edu*, which can be interpreted as follows: reading from right to left: *edu* is a domain name, preceded by the router name, in this case *utc*, preceded by the server name with the user mailbox, in this case *utcdc01*. If the server is the same as the router then the number of stems are fewer. In that case *utcdc01* would not be here. At the time mail is to be sent, the mail program on the sender computer, the POP client if it is a dial-up connection, contacts the server, commonly known as mail gateway or POP server if it is a dial-up connection, to activate the Simple Mail Transfer Protocol (SMTP) that allows the housekeeping chores like identifying itself and specifying the recipient to be completed before the mail is sent.

While the original e-mail system was designed to handle only text messages (requiring the body of the text to be in ASCII), over time and with new technologies, the new mail systems and schemes have common interfaces with graphic capabilities. MIME (Multi-Purpose Internet Mail Extension) is one such scheme invented to encode mail text into binary and can let its users choose an encoding scheme convenient to them.

Talk

The talk feature on the Internet enables two people to create a line of communication that enables them to talk to each other in real time. Normally talk software on both machines splits the screens on both computers into two parts. The top halves of the screens are for sending comments, and the bottom ones are for receiving comments. An example of talk software is WinTalk.

Internet Relay Chat (IRC)/Chat

Chat features are extensions of the talk facilities to widen the correspondence beyond two people. With chat, a group of people may engage in real-time direct correspondence where any group member's comments are broadcasted to all screens of those currently in the chat group. Chat groups are conducted in confined areas commonly known as chat rooms. One example of IRC software is the mIRC.

File Movement

File Transfer Protocol (FTP)

Internet information is stored in large databases on the Internet servers. People looking for this information can then access these servers and move information in documents as programs and data files, most often free of charge. To facilitate the transfer of programs and data files between user computers and network servers, a file transfer scheme known as file transfer protocol (FTP) is used. FTP replaced the pre-network file transfer method, which involved copying a file to a disk and physically transferring this disk to the next computer. Because of the multiplicity of computer hardware technologies on the Internet, there was a need to coordinate applications before a file was moved. This is why FTP came in — to enable transfers to be general, flexible, arbitrary and of varying file types, including the way files are stored on different computers and the representation and protection of such files during transfer. FTP transfers small documents as they are, but large files are typically compressed before being stored and transferred and are expanded once received. There are a number of application software packages to do this, including PKZIP and PKUNZIP. FTP defines and transfers documents in two file types: ASCII, which contains text characters, and binary, which uses strings of 0 and 1 to represent characters. Binary file transfers are used in all nontextual document-like programs. The user who initiates FTP is required to establish a connection to the remote computer and go through a remote login process, which may involve obtaining authorization needed for a login. Once in, the connection remains until the user closes it.

For the millions of Internet users who move programs and other documents daily, requiring individual passwords and login names by FTP servers would create a strenuous administrative job. So to permit arbitrary users access to FTP servers, a special computer account with an anonymous login name is created on the FTP server for FTP users. The users are, however, required to use their e-mail addresses as their passwords.

Anonymous FTP

Anonymous FTP is a file transfer protocol (FTP) to gain access to files stored on a remote computer, just like in the normal FTP process, except in this process your e-mail address is taken as your password and the user name is always taken as "anonymous."

Remote Access

Telnet

File Transfer Protocol on the Internet enables users to move programs and document files from Internet FTP servers to their computers and back. But because of the Internet bandwidth and traffic, sometimes it may be more beneficial not to move files from a remote computer on the Internet but to login on that computer and do the file access right there. Sometimes remote login may be caused by the need to do onsite processing of the file as a result of the availability of the required software at the site.

The remote login process is accomplished through a telnet session. The process is initiated by a user executing telnet software on his or her computer. This software then forms a remote connection. Once connected, the host computer will call for the normal login process requiring a user to provide a login name and a password. Just like in FTP, some telnet servers on the Internet allocate a special anonymous or guest account where the telnet user then logs in as a guest using only his or her e-mail address as a password.

Internet Access and Search

World Wide Web (WWW)

The World Wide Web is the newest, and fast becoming the most popular, Internet service, just behind e-mail. WWW is that feature of the Internet acting like a low depository of information organized in hypertext. A document in hypertext format may have some of its parts like words and phrases highlighted to indicate a link to other related documents that may be on other WWW servers. Clicking on the highlighted part takes the viewer to the related information.

Hypertext documents are displayed as pages. Because hypertext documents display only textual information, the WWW is more than a hypertext system; it is really a distributed hypermedia system, a superset of the hypertext, which can also display information that includes digitized photographic images, rich graphics, sound and animation. With the development of Java programming language, hypermedia is becoming the fastest growing part of the WWW. WWW documents in hypertext are created using a language known as Hypertext Markup Language (HTML). HTML allows documents created by other applications to accept guidelines for display of the documents by a browser.

A browser is a Web client program that allows a user to view Web information via menus of information resources for a particular Web site and selectable links to other related sites. Different browsers may display the same document differently. Through the Hypertext Transport Protocol (HTTP), browsers request specific items from Web servers. HTTP specifically defines the format of these requests and those of the returned documents. Browsers contain HTML interpreters to display documents returned by Web servers and to format documents sent to web servers.

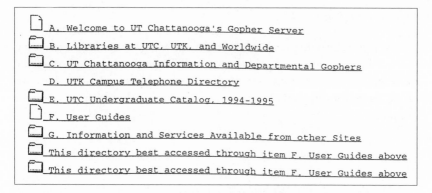

Figure 1.3 Gopher Menu

WWW browsers like Microsoft Internet Explorer and Netscape Navigator create graphical user interface (GUI) environments, meaning that they primarily display information with full use of graphics and animation.

Gopher

Gopher is an old text-based information search-and-retrieval tool developed at the University of Minnesota. It uses a simple menu system for selecting information. A gopher server stores information, and the gopher client is the program that searches for requested information on the Internet. Although it retrieves text-based information, gopher has a graphical user interface (GUI) that displays small menu folder icons before each information line indicating whether it is a file, a directory, a telnet host or a search query. See Figure 1.3. Gopher searches are limited, though, because gopher clients only search information on gopher servers.

Archie

Archie was developed in the early 1980s as an FTP indexing tool. It catalogs files on FTP servers on the Internet by file names and file descriptions, making it possible to search a file on the Internet by name or keyword in its description. Archie can be run from gopher servers, WWW browsers, and by e-mail to an Archie server; however, the easiest method is from a gopher server. Archie searches return a list of server sites where the sought file can be located.

Veronica/Jughead

Veronica and Jughead are Internet indexing tools. However, they index only information on gopher servers. Whereas Veronica lists all server titles that fit the search criteria, Jughead lists only current titles. Because of the limitations in gopher servers, Veronica and Jughead applications are limited.

WAIS/CSO/WHOIS

WAIS stands for Wide Area Information Server, CSO stands for Computing Services Office, and WHOIS comes from "Who is." All these tools are Internet search tools serving specialized interests. For example, WAIS is more versatile than Veronica, allowing Boolean searches and searching for strings beyond gopher servers. CSO and WHOIS, on the other hand, search directories of names and e-mail accounts respectively. CSO returns information like names, e-mail addresses, telephone numbers and addresses of individuals whose names are being searched on.

Finger

Finger is a communication feature that helps Internet users identify other users. There are many versions of finger giving varying degrees of user information. In Unix, for example, a finger request with a user name gives the full name of the person along with some other personal information.

Netfind

Netfind is an Internet "white pages" directory information retrieval facility. It uses SMTP, the Internet e-mail protocol and finger, which we have already discussed, to search for information. On a given name, with keywords as additional information, Netfind can return the full name, telephone number, and e-mail address of the party sought. The search, though, may take a series of choices from a list of matching domains Netfind displays as it progressively narrows the search to the final hit or miss.

Newsgroups and Discussion Groups

Among the many resources on the Internet are the flood of news from organized news wires and news from relatives and friends. To help Internet users with particular information flavor, nonreal-time Internet services, commonly known as newsgroups or discussion groups, were formed. Newsgroups are formed around related news and information about a specific topic. For example, users interested in fly-fishing may join a newsgroup on that topic.

Discussion groups are formed along the same lines as newsgroups but involve more user interaction through individual postings. There are thousands of Internet discussion and news servers that continually update news and postings from other news servers on the Internet. There are also thousands of newsgroups and discussion groups on the Internet. A user accesses a news server using special news reader software like the popular Microsoft Windows winVN. These news reader software programs use a protocol called Net News Transport Protocol (NNTP) to transfer news between servers, and the news reader then displays the news on the user computer.

There are thousands of newsgroups and discussion categories including:

1. ALT — for alternative to conventional things in life.
2. MISC — for all miscellaneous misfits outside other known groups.
3. NEWS — for newsgroups.
4. REC — for all recreational activities.
5. SCI — for all scientific activities.
6. SOC — for discussion and news about social issues.

Chapter 2

Internet Globalization and Its Effects on Societies

Although there are no exact figures for the actual global growth of the Internet, one can get a pretty good picture of the Internet's global trends and patterns from estimates available from a variety of sources. Some of these sources are the International Telecommunication Union and Tele-Geography, which measure global telecommunication diffusion; Matrix Information Directory, which monitors global networking activities; Network Wizards, which measures global Domain Name distributions; and the World Bank and United Nations, which measure global demographic, economic and social development. Current estimates show that there are as many as 16–20 million registered hosts in all major domains with an estimated global growth of both phone lines and Internet hosts between 1994 and 1995 of around 98 percent (1). This kind of growth is breathtaking, and one can assume that at least in the near foreseeable future this growth momentum will be maintained. Viewed at both local and national levels, this growth rate points to many new local and national networks forming and joining the Internet. The Internet, seen as a collection of these local and national networks, is a super network of computers and indeed a *net* cast over the globe. Under its cast the net has created and continues to create an amalgam of cultures, religions, commerce and languages among the thousands of ethnically diverse peoples of the world. Because of its nature and architecture, as a network of computers with no geographical or judicial localization, the Internet has built an infrastructure that exhibits unparalleled globalization potential and characteristics. Indeed, right from its early days, these attributes made the Internet a technological wonder of the twentieth century.

Historically, empires, kingdoms, big and small human settlements have protected themselves from foreign influences, including physical attacks, by erecting physical barriers such as the Great Wall of China and by building moats around castles and villages or by building atop high mountains, but the Internet renders all such barriers useless. The breaking of these traditional barriers around communities and nations by this new technology has resulted in the breaking down of traditional values, which for centuries have been used in business transactions, languages, culture and religion. Although the Internet is not the first technology to spill over physical boundaries — there were technologies before it, such as newsprint, ocean-going vessels, moss, radio, television, telephone and the jet plane — it has surpassed them by far in a number of areas, including scope of coverage and speed. Its effects in this new global arena are certainly unprecedented in the history of humanity. There are going to be unparalleled changes in every aspect of human life, ranging from cultural, religious, linguistic and social changes to complete amalgamation and/or annihilation of traditional cultures, religions, languages and many other ways of life. Let us look at what seems to be the beginning of this process in areas of culture, languages, commerce, cybercrime, health and education.

Culture

Individual cultures display elements of a living creature, elements such as being born, growing up and dying. Like a living thing cultures start by evolution, grow by sustaining life through acquisition of new inputs and rejection of old useless ones and eventually become either extinct or transform through amalgamation with other strong cultures. Human cultures, since prehistoric times, have evolved through migration of peoples, and this metamorphosis has increased with the advent of better communication media. For example seagoing ships opened new avenues for cultural crusaders, whose missions were to acculturate the "uncultured." Their actions speeded up either development or extinction of the host cultures and peoples. Over the years, as better communication carriers came into use, human movements increased, and so did the pressure on individual cultures. Major technological developments like print media, wireless communication, the jet plane and television have greatly influenced global cultural changes. But none of these technological breakthroughs has had the impact or the potential that the Internet has to bring about major, unprecedented changes in global cultures. Some of the reasons why the Internet has had and is likely to have far more profound effects on global cultures follow.

Participatory Nature of the Internet Technology

Users of the Internet are full participants in the communication process, unlike in previous technologies. Consider, for example, television and radio technology. Although both are mass media and can reach millions, including poor communities in remote areas, and to some extent are quite affordable (at least the radio), both are one-way media. The recipient of the message does not have the ability to participate in the dialogue initiated by the person or persons at the transmitter. This one-way nature of television and radio is also common to other technological advances that have been influencing cultures. A participatory medium such as the Internet engages more than a one-way medium, and hence its influence on those involved in the communication is likely to be greater.

Scope

All previous technologies have had either targeted or limited scope. Their covered areas are either deliberately limited by financial, political or legal means, or they are limited by geographical barriers or by the physical capabilities of the technology itself. Take television for example. Its broadcasts are still not seen in some parts of the world because of financial, political and geographical limitations, and radio broadcasts are beamed in selected places. Whereas these previous technologies have these and other limitations in coverage, the Internet has far fewer limitations. Its freedom from national politics, its nonaffiliation with any one individual interest group, and the absence of physical and jurisdictional boundaries have all made the Internet the best global outreach medium with the greatest potential to influence global cultural changes.

Individualization of Communication

Not since the postal system was invented has communication been more individualized and personalized than it is today with the Internet. Besides individualized communication, the Internet has also provided increased delivery speed so that if a message is posted at one end of the globe, it takes just a few seconds to reach the other end. With individualized communication and speed, people of different cultures can communicate and learn from one another in shorter durations than ever before.

These and other characteristics of the Internet have created a debate on global cultural changes. Although few would deny that the last couple of decades have seen a process of globalization of world cultures through television programs like American-based MTV, soap operas, videos, movies and printed materials, the heated debate around the Internet is focused on the *speed* of this process. There is already fear that North American and indeed Western European media are slowly but effectively eroding the indigenous small cultures in many parts of the world, and the process is likely to be speeded up by the Internet.

Language

The world boasts of hundreds if not thousands of languages for the many different peoples that populate it. Historically languages, as vehicles of culture, grow through acquisition, lending and borrowing of new words, and rejection of old ones. Sometimes, though, languages become extinct, and this occurs mainly because the growth of any language is mostly driven by external influences like invasion, colonization, trade and technology.

Invasion and Colonization

In the past the languages of the strong people have always been forced on the weak ones through conquests, and these languages have consequently expanded. For example, English, French and Spanish grew and expanded through colonization. Imperial languages took root in those communities that were colonized because often the colonizers used brutal means to force the indigenous populations to learn the new language and culture, sometimes to the extent of causing extinction of the indigenous languages. However, given the current global environment, this kind of technique for the propagation of individual languages is a thing of the past.

Trade

Many languages, however, have been growing due to their appeal to different cultures. Such an appeal of a language is backed by financial forces because any time there is a financial incentive, there is a "voluntary" need to learn the language of the trade. Many financial powerhouse nations have seen their languages grow internationally. However, commerce alone cannot propel rapid growth of a language; otherwise, there would be a stampede on Japanese and German language schools. But this is not the case. Commerce, however, forces individuals involved in businesses to learn the language of the trade so that they can negotiate fair, if not better, deals.

Technology

For generations advances in technology have influenced the growth of languages as people who use such technology struggle to understand the terminology and use of the technology. Newly discovered phenomena demand and create new words to describe them, and those words inevitably enter the languages as the technologies are applied in the people's lives. There are many ways those words enter the languages. Sometimes existing words take on new meanings; for example, the word *spam* has taken on new meaning since the development of e-mail. On other occasions new words are freshly minted to describe the new technology.

Besides forcing people to learn new terms and phrases in order to use the technology, technology also helps in the spread of certain languages through cultural appeal. For example, English and French, and to a lesser extent Spanish, have grown with the new technologies like television, video, magazines and now the Internet, exposing these languages to large audiences of young people in many different cultures. In fact, many people credit the phenomenal growth of English into a de facto international language of commerce and communication to technological advances in the United States. Indeed, English has become a lingua franca for the Internet because of the history and the factors influencing the growth of the Internet. According to a study by the Altis Technologies and the Internet, English has an 82.3 percent share of all languages in cyberspace (2).

Historically, the Internet, as we discussed in Chapter One, started in the United States, and many of the powers that be, which propelled the Internet to its current state, originated in the United States, a mainly English-speaking country. Now that the Internet is progressively commercially driven, many of the biggest commercial interests are from English-speaking countries. With the nature of the Internet's outreach, a certain brand of English is slowly becoming a global language of communication, propelled mainly by the Internet and commerce.

Commerce

Since the ceasing of the Internet's central guiding force the NSF, the Internet has become one global open marketplace for selling and purchasing goods and services and for exchanging information. The Internet's ability to connect people and communities globally has enabled it to create new global markets and new growth areas for many companies and businesses.

From the early days commerce done by bartering has nurtured globalization by bringing peoples and cultures together to trade for goods they like but do not have in exchange for goods that they have. Over the centuries and as technology improved, globalization through commerce picked up momentum, and with the advent of the Internet there has been a sudden jump in global commerce, which has come to be known commonly as electronic commerce or e-commerce. E-commerce has speeded up the process of globalization for a number of reasons:

1. The Internet's global outreach

    Almost every country is connected in some fashion to the Internet, with full Internet services for most and mail-only services for a few. But with the current Internet growth rate, it will be a matter of only a few years before every country will be truly on the Internet. This will open for business a potential customer base of 5 billion people.

2. Twenty-four-hour customer access

    The Internet has come to be the only business mall open 24 hours a day, seven days a week, creating an opportunity for many businesses usually hurt by seasons, holidays and night-and-day cycles.

3. Speed of response

    The Internet offers quick response times to both vendors and customers. For the customers requests are promptly replied to and orders are quickly filled. For the vendor the Internet speed may mean an increase in the number of orders filled and hence the turnover of goods. If a customer is not satisfied with the product, the short response time allows speedy resolving of grievances, which in itself generates high customer satisfaction.

4. Low business costs

Because of its military and academic beginnings, the Internet has been, and to a very large extent still is, a non capitalist's tool, offering lucrative services and business opportunities almost for free, with minimal monthly fees for connections. Large and small businesses are putting up their publications and related information on the Internet for free. Because of this information-for-free nature of the Internet, those businesses that have ventured onto the Internet have found the cost of running a business there still very low compared to other media such as television, radio and print.

5. Constant information updates

Unlike other advertising media, the Internet gives the business community the ability to constantly update information on products and services within a convenient time frame. The update may be in pricing, availability of commodities in stock and delivery times.

6. Better payment systems

Many still see Internet commerce as free-wheeling and anarchic because of its lack of coherence and enforceable regulations, the irrelevance of geopolitical boundaries, and its many wild west–like, clique-driven, bounty hunter–like payment systems. Progress, however, is being made to refine the payment system. As the Internet becomes a more attractive place to do commerce, big multinational companies are getting together to create a system that will insure secure payment systems, value-laden product contents and better and simplified transaction processes.

There are already many transaction and payment schemes on the market offering varying degrees of acceptance and security. The following table lists many of the currently known payment and transaction schemes (3).

New transaction and payment schemes, better standards and experimental metasystems that will greatly increase the bandwidth of the current Internet, creating a revolutionary new global environment for business and commerce, are on the horizon. For example, the very High-Speed Backbone Network (VBNS), connecting several U.S.-based National Science Foundation (NSF) Supercomputers, and the I-way are just a preview of things to come.

Name	Owner	Services	Electronic Account	Electronic Checks	Credit Cards	Security Protocol
BankNet	Banknet&Secure Trust Bank, plc	online bank/credit card	yes	yes		SET
BuyWay	MPACT Immedia	transaction			yes	SSL
Checkfree	Checkfree Corp.	transaction	yes	yes		SSL
Clickshare	Clickshare Service, Corp.	track movement /settle charges	yes	yes		
Commercenet	Commercenet Corp.	transactions	yes	yes	yes	SHTTP
Cybank	Cybank	payment	yes	yes		
CyberCash	CyberCash, Inc.	transactions	yes		yes	SET
CyberSource	CyberSource Corp.	real-time transaction	yes		yes	
Ecash	Digicash, Inc.	transactions	yes	yes		SSL
E-gold	Gold&Silver Reserve, Inc.	transactions	yes	yes		
Electronic Funds Clearinghouse	Electronic Fund Clearing House, Inc.	transmission	yes	yes		SSL
eVend	eVend, Inc.	transaction			yes	SSL
First Virtual	First Virtual Holdings, Corp.	payment			yes	SSL
FSTC Electronic Check	Financial Ser. Consortium of Banks	transactions	yes	yes		SSL
iWinpak	iWinpack Corp.	transactions	yes		yes	PGP
LETSystems	Letsgo Manchester	exchange	yes ("local money")			
Micro Payment Transfer Protocol (MPTP)	W3C Electronic Payment Grp.	payments	yes			SSL
Millicent	Digital Equipment	payments	yes			
Mini-Pay	IBM	payments	yes			SSL
Mondex	Mondex International	transactions	yes	yes		SSL
Neosphere Micropayment	Neosphere	transaction	yes		yes	Java
NetBank's NetCash	NetBank	transaction	yes	yes		SSL

NetBill	Carnegie-Mellon Univ.	Tran/educ.	yes	yes	yes	SSL
NetCash	Univ. of South Cal.	Tran/educ.	yes	yes	yes	SSL
NetCheque	Univ. of South Cal.	Tran/educ.	yes	yes	yes	SSL
NetFare	CUC International	payments			yes	SSL
NetMarket	Netmarket, Inc.	transactions	yes	yes		SSL
Online Check Systems	Online Check System, Inc.	payments	yes	yes		SSL
Open Market	Open Market, Inc.	payment	yes	yes	yes	SSL
Pay2See	Pay2See, Inc.	payment (to use software)			yes	SSL
Redi-Check	Redi-Check, Corp.	payment	yes	yes		SSL
Secure-Bank.Com	Secure Bank.Com	transaction	yes	yes	yes	SSL
Secure Electronic Transaction	Visa/MasterCard	transactions			yes	SSL
SecureOrder	Automated Transaction Services	transaction	yes	yes	yes	SSL
SecureTrans	Valley Internet services	transaction	yes	yes	yes	SSL
Security First Network Bank	Secure First Network Bank	transactions	yes	yes	yes	SSL
SubScrip	Univ. of Newcastle	edu/payment				
Sun Internet Commerce Group	Sun Microsystem	education/services				
VirtualPay	Virtual Pay	payment	yes	yes	yes	SSL
Ziplock	Portland Software	payment			yes	SSL

Table 1. E-commerce Payment and Transaction Schemes

Cybercrimes

The Internet globalization process has not only affected cultures, languages and commerce but has also helped the global spread of human vices commonly known as digital crimes or cybercrimes. These cybercrimes are not in any way new; they are the same old crimes, but the Internet with its global outreach and other features has provided a new environment that offers cybercriminals a global audience, faster transmission, anonymity and, in the absence of an effective, enforceable legal system, unlikely conviction.

These cybercrimes are fueled by the same fundamental business principles that have fueled the explosion of e-commerce as we have seen in the previous section because for many cybercrimes the motive is making money; there are, however, a small number of crimes perpetrated purely for mental and intellectual challenge, without any financial motives, and some that are done purely as personal vendettas. Currently most cybercrimes fall under one of the following categories:

1. Software piracy
2. Pornography (mostly child pornography)
3. Credit card fraud
4. Spooling
5. Espionage
6. E-mail misuse
7. Viruses and worms
8. System break-ins

In the next chapter we will give a more detailed description of each of these crimes.

Health (Telemedicine)

One of the greatest benefits of the Internet has probably been in medicine. Medical information delivery over the Internet, commonly known as telemedicine, is becoming one of the crown jewels of the Internet globalization process. Telemedicine is the delivery of health care and the exchange of health information such as the transfer of basic patient information, including interviews, examination and consultation reports; transfer of medical images such as radiographs, CT scans, MRIs and ultrasound; and the transfer of pathology and other medical procedure reports over mainly computer networks and other telecommunication devices.

Because of its ability to deliver medical care around the globe, telemedicine has reached remote communities and enhanced the medical services in these communities with state-of-the-art services from fully equipped usually first-rate medical centers. World Bank telecommunications director James Bond told a press conference of one incident that clearly demonstrates the value of telemedicine: a doctor in Zambia was able to treat a patient suffering from malaria, thanks to his electronic mail computer link. The doctor sent a message detailing the man's symptoms to a colleague in London, who suggested he contact an expert at the National Institute of Health in Bethesda, Maryland. The U.S. expert recognized the symptoms as belonging to a form of malaria not normally seen in Zambia and was able to tell the doctor in Zambia how to treat it (4).

Besides reaching inaccessible areas of the world, telemedicine is also being used in urban but restricted areas like prisons. In both rural and urban restricted communities, state-of-the-art and surgery procedures that need great expertise have been performed via computers and videos by specialists usually thousands of miles away from the site. Because of the excitement created by telemedicine, areas where telemedicine can be applied are no longer limited as they were in the pre–Internet days. Telemedicine's reach is now wide and is getting wider as the Internet's reach gets wider. According to Eran B. Schenker (5), there are eight application areas:

1. Networking of large healthcare groups and multicampus linking of hospitals and research centers
2. Linkages among rural health clinics to a central hospital
3. Physician-to-hospital links for transfer of patient information, diagnostic consultations and research literature
4. Use of video and satellite relay to train healthcare professionals in widely distributed or remote clinical settings
5. Transfer of diagnostic information such as electrocardiograms or X-rays
6. Videoconferencing among members of healthcare teams
7. Capturing "grand rounds" on video for use in remote consultation or training
8. Instant access to, and aided search techniques for gathering, information from databases

The benefits of telemedicine are enormous including the most obvious ones:

1. Time: Because most patients in need of medical care are either in remote or restricted areas, patient information access and the time

of delivery of such services is highly restricted, and the process is lengthy. But with integrated patient records and expert grouping offered by telemedicine, the time element is highly improved and access made easy.

2. Speed: Telemedicine greatly improves the speed of delivery of health services from minor services like consultation with a physician to complex surgeries. Services are delivered fast because there is no need for the physician, laboratory technicians and nurses to travel to and from those locations.

3. Costs: Because there is no travel of expert personnel involved or other costs typically involved in the upkeep of patients, costs are greatly reduced. This alone may be the greatest benefit from telemedicine because patients in those communities can hardly afford the expenses involved with conventional care.

Although telemedicine programs still lack basic facilities like telephone lines and experienced on-site expert personnel, the future of telemedicine looks bright and is likely to get better as the Internet develops even further.

Education

Online education is the process of delivering educational instruction services via telephone, radio, television and computer communication lines to off-site locations, usually remote ones. It includes the delivery of educational services to regions of the world usually with nonexisting infrastructures and to urban restricted areas like prisons via the Internet and related telecommunication technologies. It also includes delivery of education services to not-so-remote and restricted areas where there are no facilities due to other reasons besides remoteness. Virtual universities are being set up to bring university education to areas where it is not financially feasible to have traditional structures. For example, with the help of the Internet, the World Bank has launched a "Cyber University" called the African Virtual University (AVU), initially connecting seven countries, with a planned expansion to connect most of the African countries. The AVU network uses high-quality compressed digital video uplinked to satellites. The signals are then transmitted from Europe and the United States and are received through local ground campus satellite dishes. When fully operational, AVU will link member university libraries and at the same time bring live class interaction between students and instructors thousands of miles apart. AVU is expected to greatly enhance the quality of education in those countries and to bring the continent's quality of science and technology education up to par with that of Europe and North America (6).

With rapid advances in technology and the changing workplace, education has come center stage. Technological advancements, particularly the Internet, have had a great impact on education, making it available to those who might otherwise not have it. Several tools are used to deliver online education:

1. Simple e-mail: this is what instructors use as needed and students use the same to keep in touch with their instructors and classmates.

2. Shared resources like electronic chalkboards: the Instructors use electronic chalkboards, and the students, sometimes scattered in remote areas, view the electronic inscription on their computer terminals or television receivers.

3. Shared databases: This is where students and instructors can exchange class assignments, notes, course materials and any other form of communication.

4. Chartboards: this is where students and sometimes their instructors can exchange scholastic information.

The results are likely to be profound. Just like telemedicine, online education has the potential to transform global education instruction, process and delivery as we know it today by bringing standards, quality, affordability and resources where such services wouldn't have been possible just a few years before the Internet.

Chapter 3

The Internet as a
Global Medium: Concerns

In the previous chapter we discussed the benefits of the phenomenal growth of the Internet in terms of globalization. Although the benefits are many and humanity is grateful to Internet technology and has embraced it in droves, this unprecedented expansion of the Internet has also unquestioningly provided a cozy environment for old crimes to flourish. In particular, it has provided a new set of temptations that make the committing of these old crimes more convenient and less conspicuous, thus a lot easier. Richard Rubin outlines seven of these temptations as follows (1):

1. Speed

    Both computer and telecommunication technology have greatly increased the speed of transmission of digital data, which means that one can violate common decency concerning transmission of such data speedily and not get caught in the act. Also, the act is over before one has time to analyze its consequences or one's guilt.

2. Privacy and Anonymity

    If no one witnesses a questionable act one has committed, then there is little or no guilt on the doer's part. Privacy and anonymity, both of which can be easily attained using this new technology, support this weakness, enabling one to create what can be called "moral distancing" from one's actions.

3. Nature of Medium

The nature of storage and transmission of digital information in the digital age is different in many aspects from that of the Gutenberg print era. The electronic medium of the digital age permits one to steal information without actually removing it. This virtual ability to remove and leave the original "untouched" is a great temptation to us, creating an impression on us that nothing has been stolen.

4. Aesthetic Attraction

Humanity is endowed with a competitive zeal to achieve far beyond our limitations. So we naturally feel a sense of accomplishment whenever we break down the efforts of our opponents or the walls of the unknown. This sense of accomplishment brings about a creative pride whenever not-so-well-known creative individuals come up with elegant solutions to technological problems. This fascination and sense of accomplishment create an exuberance among hackers that ignores the value and the importance of the information attacked and justifies the action itself.

5. Increased Availability of Potential Victims

There maybe a sense of amusement and ease in knowing that with just a few key strokes one's message and action can be felt over wide areas and by millions of people. Unfortunately, this sense can very easily turn into evil feelings as soon as one realizes the power he or she has over the millions of invisible and unsuspecting people.

6. International Scope

The global outreach of the Internet creates an appetite for more of whatever one is doing because the greater the coverage, the greater the monetary, economic and political incentives. The ability to cover the globe and to influence an entire geopolitical world while making plenty of money sometimes blinds individuals to social and ethical issues associated with their actions.

7. The Power to Destroy

According to Robert Marsh, chairman of the Commission on Critical Infrastructure Protection, an agency set up by President Clinton to look into the vulnerability of the United States to a computer attack, a computer attack could shut down the nation's communication power grids. "The potential for disaster is real and the time to act is now," says Marsh (2).

This list summarizes the destructive capacity of information technology and the dangers associated with computer technology if it falls into the wrong hands. Unfortunately these individuals can do anything for money, glory, fame or for just mere exhilaration. Most people who have heard about Internet crimes are amazed and mesmerized by them, thereby complicating the efforts to fight such crimes, since these criminals are admired as wiz kids. This is a battle we still have to fight.

In addition to rejuvenating old crimes, the new technology has also given rise to cybercrimes popularly referred to as "digital crimes." Throughout this chapter we are going to examine these digital crimes, and the concerns arising from them, without suggesting solutions. My goal is to create awareness and bring about a discussion of these issues. The reader is encouraged to find other problems not discussed here and help to initiate a search for solutions.

Digital Crimes

A thorough study of Rubin's temptations helps us understand the types of Internet crimes and psychology of the cybercriminals. We can profile a cybercriminal based on the position of the crime on the Internet crime spectrum. On one end of this spectrum are crimes meant to generate money for the criminal, and on the other end are those crimes intended for the sole purpose of intellectual challenge. These criminals, therefore, range from disgruntled and former employees, software developers, professionals with a financial motive, and terrorists, to supposedly "innocent" pranksters. We will try to do a limited criminal profiling for these crimes as we survey the current major Internet or digital crimes.

Unauthorized Access to Computer Systems

Computer system break-in is one of the most common and best-known digital crimes. Unfortunately system break-ins are complex crimes that make criminal profiling difficult and apprehension rare because there are as many break-ins as there are motives.

Motives

Computer system break-ins are committed for various reasons:
1. Financial benefits
    This is perhaps the most common reason for computer system break-ins that are done mostly by insiders, people who have some idea

of using the information to get them to the money, usually through extortion and ransom. Most criminals in this category are seasoned employees who have considerable experience in using software/information they're trying to steal, and they know exactly what to do with the information. This information is often either sold to competing companies or used for extortion. The information stolen in this category is mostly vital and value laden and can fetch substantial personal benefit, mostly financial or custodial.

2. Theft of services

Intruders break into computer systems and, without taking or destroying anything in the system, just use the system for personal work and then leave, most times without detection. A number of crimes can be committed this way because the intruder is difficult to trace, unless caught in the act. Companies lose a lot of money this way because resources worth billions of dollars are used without being paid for. More seriously, life-threatening crimes can be committed using stolen resources. Many criminals in this category are young, highly motivated and very knowledgeable about the resources available on the victim's computers, and they know how to use the resources once obtained.

3. Data and information alteration

In this instance, the intruder either destroys data on the system or alters it. This kind of crime is done mostly by disgruntled employees or ex-workers who are trying to pay back someone or the company for what they perceive as mistreatment they have received. There are various ways data can be altered:

•Alteration with recovery. After a duration or after certain conditions are met, the altered data returns to its original form. The duration and conditions required depend on a number of things as spelled out by the criminal.

•Partial alteration. Several portions of the files are permanently altered, but the bulk of the data is recoverable. The recovery conditions of the files also depend on the conditions set by the criminal.

• Time bomb. This is self-destruction of information after a certain period of time unless certain conditions spelled out by the criminal are met.

• Complete destruction. Information is completely destroyed without any stated conditions. This kind of destruction is done mostly by ex-employees who are not seeking financial gain but may be paying back their former employers, whom they hold responsible for their loss of job. It may also be done by ex-employees trying to destroy incriminating evidence. Sometimes current employees can also get involved in these kinds of acts. They may want to pay back employers who have denied or delayed their promotion, or they may suspect that somebody is on their tracks and that the only way to cover up evidence is to destroy all the information.

4. Intellectual challenge

Although a majority of computer system break-ins are done as vendettas or for financial gain, a small percentage are done for purely mental challenge, mostly by young people. These types of crimes are committed by highly intelligent individuals for the thrill of mental stimulation. Most times the intruders just want to send out a "signal" to the computer systems owner that they are around and that they can do better. The majority of the criminals in this category are either young people or activists. For example, a number of U.S. Federal agencies' Web pages have recently been visited this way and have fallen victim to these kinds of crimes.

Although system break-ins are considered one of the most frequent digital crimes, they are the least reported. According to Ian Davis, 85 to 97 percent of all system break-ins are never detected (3). However, even of the few that get detected, a far smaller percentage is reported, the main reasons being that many system administrators pay little to no attention to system security, and those who do, do not have enough resources to prevent what many see as a never-ending, very expensive problem that rarely occurs. Additionally, many companies fear the bad image that may result from publicizing such incidents, exposing in the process both system weaknesses and management incompetence.

Types of Break-ins

Criminals, mostly hackers, gain access to computer systems through a variety of means, including remote logins, using personal and custom software and a little bit of wizardry, and actual physical break-in, using knowledge of the equipment and premises. There are several types of computer system break-ins:

1. IP Spoofing

IP spoofing involves doping one computer to electronically disguise itself as another computer, most often a server, and in so doing gaining access to the doped computer. Once in, the criminal has un-limited access to the resources of the computer broken into.

2. Password Sniffing

Besides spoofing, intruders also employ software programs to mon-itor intercomputer communication in the network to pick up and record user passwords and other related information that is later used to break into the system. This scheme is called password sniffing.

3. Trial and Error

This is the guessing of a password by trying all possible combi-nations of a password. Eventually with patience, the password is hit and the intruder gains access to the system. One solution to this problem is to make the process of guessing passwords very long and time consuming so that it frustrates the would-be intruder. It is also helpful for the system to lock after a couple of trials. In most sensi-tive computer systems, after a few trials a warning signal is sent to a monitoring center.

4. Trash Mining

Many times we discard vital information, usually scattered on bits and pieces of paper, as trash. Trash can be a source of valuable infor-mation to information sleuths. Things like social security and phone numbers and other personal information usually on old mail, personal papers, scheduling books and ordinary receipts are discarded as trash. To the criminals trash is a gold mine of information.

5. Trap Doors

Trap doors are loopholes often intentionally left in application and system programs to routinely let programmers and system designers in to debug any problems that may arise while the programs are in use; they can also provide access to vital information about indi-viduals and organizations. Usually program designers assume that nobody else will ever know of the existence of these trap doors; how-ever, this is not always the case.

6. Wiretapping of Communication Lines

Many times communication lines are not secure, and intruders can with little effort listen in and get all the information they need for free. With new technologies they can even listen in from across the street.

7. Internet Web-sitting

New Web-based programs can migrate to remote client comput-ers and gather information on the user's computer, including files in other directories on the user's computer. This can give the intruder quick and easy access to vital information.

Pornography

To understand the coinducive and convenient environment created by the Internet for the pornographic industry, one has to understand the way all digital pictures are transported on the Internet. As we saw in Chapter One, information on the Internet is transported as streams of zeros and ones grouped into packets. A single message does not have to travel in a single packet, which means that a single message can be broken into several packets. All these packets from a single message do not have to travel in a specific route in the network; individual packets can take different paths as long as they arrive at the intended recipient computer. At the receiving computer, the packets are then reassembled to recover the original message. This means that a pornographic picture and a picture of a rose, when both are broken into packets and sent to their respective destinations, can take any route, intermingling and remaining, indistinguishable until they reach their respective final destinations. Remember that in the real world, transporting of pornographic materials through postal systems is illegal, and of course it is easy to see a pornographic picture if it is intercepted. However, this is not possible on the Internet until the message reaches its destination. To those in the pornographic industry, transportation of pornography is now the least of their problems in their expanding business.

Criminals have used this feature of the Internet, together with its global outreach, to distribute pornographic materials over the Internet. The anonymity feature of the Internet, where Internet postings can be sent via an anonymous server stripped of its identity before it is sent further on its way, has further complicated the fight against Internet pornography.

Another complication in this unending and heated debate about Internet pornography is the muddle created by the Internet on the free-speech issue. During the print era it was easy to fight pornography in print or video form because the domains where it thrived were clear and known. They were print materials, movies and video cassettes. It was easy to protect the young, and we had redefined the techniques of policing the distribution channels. For example no children below a certain age group were allowed in R-rated movies or allowed to rent R-rated materials from rental stores. In short, there were laws on the books to fight pornography, and there was a definite profile of those trading in pornography. With the Internet, however, the rules of the game are far different and are not coherent. One can, for example, order live pornographic materials in the privacy of one's own home, can pick and select materials that fit one's fantasies, and most important, one can use the materials in any way one likes without anybody knowing about it and without publicly breaking any law. These Internet characteristics have propelled the pornographic industry into new and uncharted territories and have been a bonanza for this industry. Revenues have never been higher, and the number of new businesses is rising sharply. Although there is as yet no comprehensive study of the Internet pornographic industry to support these observations, a controversial study, recently done at Carnegie Mellon University by Marty Rimm, supports these observations. Rimm's study, entitled "Marketing Pornography on the Information Superhighway" (4), intended to give a better understanding of the actual nature of Internet pornography and looked at four categories of Internet pornography:

1. Paraphilia which includes among others transvestites, sadomasochism, voyeurism, and incest
2. Pedophilia, which includes nude pictures of young children and hardcore sex acts involving young children
3. Hard-core, which includes explicit sexual contacts between two or more individuals
4. Soft-core, which includes nude and seminude human figures, usually emphasizing their physical features like breasts and genitalia with no physical contacts

For each category the study focused on three issues: content availability, who is involved, and what is popular. Among the major findings as reported by Philips Elmer-Dewitt are (5)

1. that there is a high volume of porno materials in the form of pictures, stories, descriptions and video clips;
2. that online pornographic materials are big moneymakers, this money being mainly from adults who are frequent visitors to computer bulletin board systems (BBSs), where they are charged membership fees of up to $40 per month;
3. that online pornographic materials are extremely popular, ranking among the most popular adult online recreational entertainment materials;
4. that it is a man's pastime (men form an overwhelming percentage of visitors to these sites, whereas women visitors were a mere 2%);

5. that the materials found were of a deviant sexual nature like bondage and sadomasochism, mostly those outside the mainstream print medium and were mostly made up of naked women.

However, the findings of the study, although still very preliminary and controversial, may help to redefine the porno-criminal profiles for law enforcement agents. What is even more disturbing is the shattering of all the principles upon which we had built the profiles of a porno criminal.

Software Piracy

Software piracy, the illegal copying of computer software, is one of the oldest computer crimes. It was high up the list even before the popularity of the Internet hit the news media. In the early 1970s software was not protected in the sense of intellectual property rights as we know it today. Back then computer owners and users used to meet in user groups and exchange the latest software among members. The actual protection of software did not begin until the Computer Copyright Act of 1980, which defined software as a "literary" work, therefore, placing it under the protection of the copyright laws. However, this definition has not fully encompassed all computer issues; thus protection muddles are still experienced today. Although we cannot trace the origins of software piracy, we can say that it started with the development of the floppy and hard disk technology. Software piracy is a catch phrase involving many aspects of software, from duplication beyond normal user-backup copies through distribution on the Internet in violation of copyright and patent laws. In general, however, there are five distinguishable forms of software piracy (5):

1. Owner Distribution

    Under owner distribution the buyer of the software makes numerous copies beyond the legal number of backup copies, usually intending to distribute them either for free or to make money.

2. Dealer Deal

    The dealer deal involves a dealer making an incredible deal to the buyer of free software loaded on the purchased product. The software is usually loaded on a hard disk with no original disks given to the buyer.

3. Counterfeiting

    This is where thousands of copies of the original are made and fraudulently sold, usually below market value, as legitimate originals. The counterfeits are usually exact look-alikes of the genuine software.

4. Internet Distribution
   This involves the downloading of copyrighted software off the Internet free or almost free, usually from a bulletin board.
5. Rental Software Lifting
   This is a scheme involving renting a computer system with needed software. Once the system is in the criminal's hands, he or she copies as much software as needed and then returns the system to the renting agency.

Piracy is the leading problem for the software industry, effecting a revenue drain both in lost sales and in attempts at prevention. According to the latest figures by *Investors Business Daily* (6), the value of pirated software in 1996 was $11.2 billion, involving an estimated 250 million software units pirated globally. The problem, however, is being dealt with on all fronts, both by governments and by the private sector (mainly the software industry),through enforcement of software protection laws that are on books in many countries. The efforts seem to be working because the rate of pirating software is declining, having crested in 1995.

E-mail Nonsense

Since the dawn of the Internet, e-mail service has been its crown jewel, and even in the age of graphic animated images, e-mail is still the largest service of the Internet. Almost every Internet user has an e-mail account. But even though a large percentage of Internet traffic is useful e-mail, there is a growing problem of e-mail *spam*. Spam is the flooding of the Internet's e-mail address boxes with unwanted and unsolicited e-mails. There are three types of spams:

1. E-mail bombs
   This involves an e-mail program that the sender attaches to one or more e-mail messages before sending them to a specified e-mail box. Upon arrival, the program causes the attached mail to explode, in the process generating thousands of similar messages. This explosion of messages overwhelms the e-mail account server, causing it to crash (6).
2. Junk mail
   Junk mail is unwanted and unsolicited mail. As the Internet expands and many businesses join, the Internet is becoming a gold mine for some businesses involved in advertising. Such businesses get individual e-mail addresses by spoofing the Internet, especially

Usenet newsgroups and specialty Internet groups. This they do by subscribing to thousands of these lists with only one motive: to steal user lists. Sometimes they collect user addresses by using of cookie programs. There are also other companies that, through their Web sites, require visitors to visit these sites to register before they are let in. By doing this those companies collect thousands of e-mail addresses, which they eventually sell to advertisers. Other sources of e-mail addresses are public places like universities, public institutions, company Web sites and millions of personal Web sites. It is becoming common for one e-mail address box to receive close to five thousand e-mails a day.

3. Usenet Spam

Usenet spam involves downloading one message to selected Usenet servers to be sent to every member of that host. This kind of spam is aimed at getting to that server's user lists, but such action ends up clogging the server mail system. Of late, advertisers have also started to use this technique of collecting e-mail addresses.

Spamming is bad because it creates problems for almost every Internet user through added expenses and additional time spent in deleting all the unwanted mail (7). And according to John Levine it is also bad because (7)

1. those who are involved in sending spam mainly for advertising get a free ride because their expenses are paid by the recipient through time spent identifying and discarding the mail and additional changes that may accrue because some Internet service providers (ISPs) limit the number of e-mails subscribers can get without charge.
2. many spammers, in order to avoid blocking by Internet systems managers, go via innocent intermediate systems that do not yet have brokers so that once through one server, they cannot be blocked any more. This quite often creates chaos at these servers, with space and time spent dealing with unwanted messages;
3. many spammers use unauthorized endorsements of whatever they are advertising from unsuspecting names usually taken off Internet groups and claim that the owner of the name has used the product and makes the stated endorsement of the product. All these are of course lies.

It takes effort to get off spammers' lists. In fact, sometimes trying to send a "remove" request may end up putting the sender's e-mail address on more spammers' lists. However, there are several ways to block spams,

including filtering at an individual e-mail account and blocking spams at
the system manager's level on the LAN and at the ISP level. ISPs have also
started taking spammers to court. For example, America Online won an
injunction against Cyber Promotions, Inc., and another against Over the
Air Equipment; both companies are bulk e-mail advertisers (8).

Internet Fraud

With the estimated U.S. $100 billion in Internet commerce by the
year 2000, Internet fraud is similarly expected to rise (9). As Internet commerce picks up momentum, industry experts and financial institutions,
especially credit card companies, are bracing themselves for a rise in Internet fraud by devising secure ways of doing Internet transactions. The following types of Internet fraud are particularly being targeted:

1. Cyberpayments

    This is an area most susceptible to fraud. There are claims from
    Internet security experts that the current Internet security protocol
    used in payments is not secure enough because the cryptography still
    used is too easy to decode and difficult to upgrade (10). With the cur-
    rent encryption standards and Internet payment methods and the lack
    of universally accepted secure payment and transmission standards,
    it is likely that someone can eavesdrop on the Internet transmission
    and spoof credit card and other sensitive information. Noting that
    the growth of Internet commerce depends on secure payment meth-
    ods, a number of companies are racing to come up with secure pay-
    ment schemes like those discussed in chapter two.

2. Dubious Merchants

    A number of dubious companies claiming to be doing legitimate
    businesses have opened shop on the Internet. These companies adver-
    tise products they do not have. Once a customer makes a selection
    and decides to pay by credit card, the product bought never arrives,
    yet payments are taken out of the customer's account. Dubious mer-
    chants are difficult to trace because they have no permanent addresses.
    However, some states in the United States, like California, have
    passed regulations that require cybermerchants to tell their customers
    how to find them by listing their street address on their Web sites.

3. Substandard Products

    The old trickster method used by telemarketers is in use again on
    the Internet, where merchants post and promise high-class merchan-

dise on Web sites and then deliver substandard ones. Many of these merchants are difficult to reach for complaint and are also difficult to track down by law enforcement because, for one thing, many may be offshore, where state and national laws cannot reach them. Even those in one country keep on moving, leaving no traceable addresses.

4. Other Schemes

The Internet has become a new playground for all types of telemarketing scams like pyramids, swindling, bogus services and all known get-rich-quick schemes. Although online credit card scams have received the most attention lately, there are many other scams where scam artists promise quick profits on their Web sites and then wait for would-be investors to pour in money. Sometimes scam artists pose as ISPs and tell users that they are reconfiguring the system and they want to confirm the user's registration information, which includes credit card numbers and social security numbers and e-mail addresses.

Net Gambling

Gambling is not a new pastime. For many communities gambling has, over the years, become socially acceptable because many community leaders use it as a way of raising money. In the United States alone all but 13 states have one or more official lotteries, raising revenue from gaming and waging to U.S. $482 billion in 1994, an increase of 22 percent over a year before (11). In fact, in the United States alone Internet gaming took in more money in 1994 than traditional slot machines, and the industry is expected to reach U.S. $400 billion per year by the year 2000. A growing number of gambling links display colorful Web sites with dazzling animated graphics and offer different computer games like roulette, blackjack, baccarat, slots, poker and craps. And in many other parts of the world gambling is legal, but pre–Internet-era gambling was regulated by a set of laws so that the innocent and young were not affected by it. This is not the case with Internet gambling, which, like Internet pornography, affects all people, regardless of age and is difficult to regulate.

The Internet has resurrected gambling in the same way it did pornography — by making it more easily accessible, more exclusive, and more global. However, as in the case of pornography, in so doing, it has created more problems for society. For example offshore gambling companies have increased tremendously in the last couple of years. Many of these gambling sites located offshore are like ministates not bound by any national law from outside. They can, therefore, play spoiler for any nation serious about the vices of gambling by allowing people living in nations where gambling is illegal to gamble in the privacy of their own homes.

Internet Information Gathering — Espionage

Since the birth of the Internet, digital information gathering has taken a new turn. The Internet is like a huge leaking vessel of information, and anybody with the knowledge of where to look can collect. Teams of self-styled information sleuths comb the Internet for information either to sell or hold for ransom. While public debates rage about the invasion of individual privacy and security by Internet sleuths, a covert war is being waged by corporations and governments around the globe to curb this information leakage.

In fact in the United States, according to John Deutch, CIA director (12), the growing threat of cyberspace attack is ranked among the top five threats the U.S. military is preparing for that may involve military, industrial and commercial records. U.S. national security fears are focused on three main areas:

1. Military Espionage

    This may involve the passing of military information to foreign powers, most times for financial rewards. The Internet is making this process a lot easier.

2. Industrial Espionage

    Industrial espionage may involve the passing of industrial information to foreign companies. Since the end of the cold war, industrial espionage has grown to alarming proportions, as many of the old military spies simply changed gloves and locations.

3. Cyberwarfare

    This involves real information attacks on military, industrial and financial databases, rendering them useless. As nations become more and more dependent on information, the security of that information is becoming a primary goal of national security strategy. Centers of paramount importance could include air traffic control systems, power plants, financial institutions (including the Federal Reserve and the stock exchange), fund transfer centers and military installations.

Such attacks may not originate from organized governments and powers but may even start with small bands of individuals having a good understanding of the working of the Internet. The fear of a cyberattack on the United States is so real that a Commission on Critical Infrastructure Protection was set up to investigate possible dangers of such cyberterrorism so as to protect the targets, anticipate the methods likely to be used, and come up with a possible defense strategy. The committee's report was delivered to the president in late October 1997, with classified findings as recommendations to prevent a catastrophic computer attack that might shut down communications and power grids. The committee recommended stepping up research and establishing nationwide programs to educate people on the scope of the problem and revising existing laws to ensure protection against electronic attacks through the Internet (13).

Although the recommendations were classified, most security experts think that the recommendations are probably based on three fundamental principles:

1. Decentralization of air traffic control systems into independent systems so that the disabling of one need not bring the whole system down
2. Isolation of power circuits so that each power system and type uses different carrier lines
3. Extensive use of updated cryptography in all forms of communications (14)

A generation of new encryption standards could make code breaking extremely difficult for would-be attackers and other cybersleuths. Another approach being taken by many governments is to train police and other law enforcement agents in cybersleuthing so that they know the tricks of the trade.

Concerns

The frequent occurrence of digital crimes has prompted the public to reexamine traditional issues of privacy, anonymity, security, censorship and health that have come under attack as a result of the new technology.

Privacy

Definition

Privacy can be defined as a right to be left alone. According to Kenneth C. Laudon, privacy is a "moral claim of individuals to control the flow of information about themselves, a social value enshrined in binding contracts like constitutions, a political statement reflected in law, and a behavioral reality reflected in the day to day routines" (14). However, the forces of technological advances are eroding these cherished values by attacking the very core: individual control over the flow of information about oneself. This individual control of the flow of personal information has two components:

1. control of external influence by having the right to
   •be left alone without disturbances
   •not be monitored
   •have no public personal identity, and
2. control of personal information including the right to dissemination of that information.

Traditionally, privacy as a custodian of the three basic elements of human existence — personal identity, individual autonomy, and a necessity for social relationships, has always been valuable, but it has gained tremendously more value in the information age because information is the most precious commodity of this new technology.

Personal Identity. Because information has become so precious, individuals are compelled to guard their personal identities from bounty hunters. Unfortunately, because of advances in technology, especially computer technology, intrusion and unauthorized access to personal information has become extremely easy, making the protection of personal identity extremely difficult. There are several avenues through which individual personal identity can be stolen, including personal checks, ATM cards, passports, drivers' licenses and social security numbers.

Autonomy. Autonomy, according to philosopher Immanuel Kant, is a kind of self-determination in which will as a practical reason both legislates the moral law and executes decisions out of a rational respect for the moral law (15). It entails the right to live in peace, to speak freely and to protect one's property, and it puts individuals in control of their destiny. However, this feeling of one's being in control of one's destiny is undermined by how much information others have about that individual. The more personal information people have about an individual, the less autonomous that individual can be, especially in decision making. As a result other people may challenge one's autonomy, depending on the quality, quantity, and value of information they possess about that individual. Although humans are social animals, they pick and choose whom to associate with, depending on the autonomy they perceive they have.

Social Relationships and Associations. Individuals in the early stages of relationships try to gather as much information as possible about their partners and then use this information to decide whether to enter into further commitment. In making personal relationship decisions, one may at times find that knowing less about an individual is better than having a lot of information on that person. There are some cases, however, in which it is better to know as much as possible. Whatever the case, the fate of such a relationship or association depends on the quantity and quality of information known and available to the decision maker.

Privacy Under Attack

A million-dollar question is how private are our lives in the information age? The answer has evaded us thus far. We can reword the question by noting that the advent of the Internet has accelerated the erosion of individual privacy, but how far has the Internet contributed to this erosion? Let us try to answer the second question by looking at areas where the Internet has effectively influenced and accelerated attacks on individual privacy.

Electronic Surveillance. At a small day care center in Connecticut parents need not worry about what their children are doing when they are away at work because these parents, if they decide, can *see* almost everything their kids are doing at any moment. This breakthrough program, called "I see you, you see me" uses the Internet together with miniature video cameras installed in the day care center that feed the pictures into the center's computer, which then feeds the pictures to the Internet. Parents with Internet connections can then "watch" their little ones live. This is probably one of the few areas where electronic surveillance is used to benefit parents affected by nationwide reports of day care child abuse. However, the program illustrates the potential of the Internet as a conduit to electronic surveillance. Now with well-placed and hidden cameras, workers can be *seen* from thousands of miles away through the electronic eye. Already surveillance cameras are mounted in law enforcement cars, and very soon they will be in homes of parents involved in child custody disputes, in homes of married couples in divorce disputes, and God knows where else. The most privacy-buster eyes are probably those in the workplace, where individual employees are closely monitored for performance. Already this skyrocketing use of workplace surveillance has raised concerns in labor organizations, work labor groups and health and privacy advocacy groups.

Software Surveillance. Computer networks, including the Internet, intranets, and LANS, are increasingly being used to expand the role and use of monitoring software installed on workers' computers to monitor their performance. These programs are rapidly gaining widespread use by agencies ranging from law enforcement to investment houses. The programs can tell one everything from how long a computer is used and for what, to what Web sites were visited or are being visited and for how long. Many times these programs also measure the actual work put in by each employee.

E-mail Monitoring. E-mail privacy issues are best illustrated by the 1993 federal ruling that barred the Bush administration from destroying mountains of computer tapes with e-mail messages dating back to President Reagan's White House correspondence (16). Although the ruling was applauded by numerous legal experts and historians, it raised many fundamental privacy issues, one being, who owns the e-mail received at work?

The ruling seemed to shatter assumptions that any e-mail is private. In a number of rulings, courts have enforced the position that supervisors have a right to read everything on company-owned computers because this reading is considered an *inside* interception of electronic messages and, therefore, is not covered by the U.S. Electronic Communication Privacy Act of 1986, which prohibits interception of *outside* electronic messages.

Public Records. When the Oregon Department of Motor Vehicle records showed up on the Internet, besides raising hair for a number of Oregonians, it also raised the fundamental issue of electronic access to public records (17). Public records in courthouses across the country are getting out of the manila files into electronic databases, together with information in insurance, law firms, and other areas. Once this information is on the Internet, anybody can get it, and whoever wants to know what car you drive, how many tickets you have, and anything else about you will. The growth of electronic networks, particularly the Internet and the corresponding growth of large databases containing personal information from financial to medical records, has made it easy and fast to share and match data records from a variety of sources including, credit card companies, records companies, court record, and a number of government agencies. The most danger raised by data sharing and record matching is in transmission of "false" and/or erroneous data on individuals. Erroneous data, once recorded in one database, gets transmitted to hundreds of other databases, forming chains of *stale* information about the individual; it becomes difficult to trace the source of the error, let alone correct it. To ease these worries, a number of credit reporting and other private information companies are letting in private individuals to check their records for accuracy. This access allows consumers to determine whether there are errors in their personal profiles. If errors are found, consumers can get those errors removed before it is too late.

Privacy Protection

Let us ponder the question of privacy protection. How can we, in this digital age where every speck of dust can be seen, protect our cherished private information and yet remain full and sane members of the information society? There are several avenues one can use to achieve a high degree of, though not total, protection. Most of these avenues are outlined by Laudon, and we discuss those here (14).

1. Use of common law

    Common law can be thought of as a body of laws developed by courts in individual cases. In many instances common law can be thought of as a rough characterization of the use of precedents by earlier courts in the administration of justice. Common law protects individual privacy through four torts:

    •Intrusion on solitude
    •Public disclosure of private facts
    •Publicly placing a person in a false light
    •Appropriation of a person's name or likeness for commercial purposes.

2. Use of national constitutions

    In many national constitutions individual privacy is protected by the supreme law of the land. Even in constitutions that do not mention directly individual privacy, there are often amendments like the First, Fourth, Ninth, and Fourteenth in the U.S. Constitution to enshrine this right.

3. Use of government statutes

    National and local governments frequently enact statutes that protect individual privacy rights. Such statutes protect individuals from both government and private intrusion. For example, the U.S. federal government has the following acts regulating the collection, dissemination and use of personal information (18):

    1. Freedom of Information Act, 1968, as Amended (5 USC 552).
    2. Fair Credit Reporting Act of 1970.
    3. The Privacy Act (1974): regulates federal government agency record keeping and disclosure practices. The Act allows most indi-

viduals to seek access to federal agency records about themselves and also requires that personal information in agency files be accurate, complete, relevant and timely.

4. Family Educational Right and Privacy Act (1974): requires schools and colleges to grant students or their parents access to student records and limits disclosure to third parties.

5. Tax Reform Act (1976): restricts disclosure of tax information for nontax purposes.

6. Right to Financial Privacy Act (1978): provides bank customers the privacy of financial records held by banks and other financial institutions.

7. Electronic Funds Transfer Act (1978): requires institutions providing EFT to notify customers about third-party access to customer accounts.

8. Privacy Protection Act (1980): prevents unannounced searches by authority of press offices and files if no one in the office is suspected of committing a crime.

9. Federal Managers Financial Integrity Act (1982).

10. Cable Communications Policy Act (1984).

11. The Electronic Communication Act (1986): broadens the protection of the 1968 Omnibus Crime Control and Safe Streets Act to include all types of electronic communications.

12. The Computer Matching and Privacy Protection Act (1986): sets standards for U.S. federal government computer matching programs, excluding matches done for statistical, law enforcement, tax and certain other causes.

13. Computer Security Act (1987).

14. The Video Privacy Protection Act (1988): prohibits video rental stores from disclosing which films a customer rents or buys.

15. Driver's Privacy Protection Act (1994): prohibits the release and use of certain personal information from state motor vehicle records.

16. The Telecommunication Act (1996): deregulates the cable and telephone companies.

17. The Medical Records Privacy Protection Act (1996):
    a. recognizes that individuals possess a right of privacy with respect to personally identifiable health information;
    b. provides that this right of privacy may not be waived in the absence of meaningful and informed consent; and

    c. provides that, in the absence of an express waiver, the right to privacy may not be eliminated or limited except as expressly provided in this act.

4. Use of market forces

Laudon also suggests the use of market forces to safeguard privacy. His market-based mechanisms are based on individual ownership of personal information and a national information market in which individuals can trade in their personal information for a fair market value. The benefit of this approach is to strengthen individual control over personal information.

Anonymity

Anonymity is the lack of identity. There are two basic types of anonymity: pseudoidentity and true anonymity.

1. Pseudoidentity: This is where an individual is identified by a certain pseudonym or number like many writers are when they take on pen names. However, if there is reason for a true identity to be revealed, the pseudoidentity can be lifted under certain circumstances.

2. True anonymity: This is where one is not known by any name including pseudonames. True anonymity is very difficult to achieve and even when achieved may have lasting consequences both good and bad. For example, it is good to have true anonymity when there is a legitimate cause or threat that needs to be reported and there is fear of reprisal, like in cases of whistle-blowing, violence and hate crimes. However, true anonymity can also be used in many undesirable ways, like in sending hate mail.

The Internet has provided fertile ground for anonymity in both categories. With no political, cultural or judicial boundaries, the Internet has provided the best facilities and assurances of anonymity through:

1. E-mail

With advances in both e-mail hardware and software, e-mail has become the most popular form of anonymity commonly referred to as pseudoanonymity. Through anonymous remailer servers, the sender of the anonymous e-mail is provided with a unique alias e-mail address and the email is stripped of its original header addresses before it is forwarded on to its destination. The message could be replied to through the alias address.

2. Postings

   Another popular anonymity channel is the use of postings on Internet newsgroups and usergroups. Anonymity to newsgroups posting is assured through the use of data transmission protocols like Simple Mail Transfer Protocol (SMTP) and Network News Transfer Protocol(NNTP), which accepts messages to servers with arbitrary field information.

3. Electronic Commerce

   In electronic commerce the debate about anonymity still rages. In some areas that have grown tremendously with the growth of the Internet, like fund transfers, anonymity is crucial for the efficient working of the system. However, transparency is needed at the same time, mostly to ensure responsibility and accountability and to prevent criminals from taking over the system.

Security

Security is an act to prevent unauthorized access, use, alteration and theft of property and physical damage to property. In general it is a state of being free from fear, worry and danger. It involves three elements:

1. Confidentiality: to prevent use of unauthorized disclosure of information to a third party; including the disclosures of personal information like medical, financial, student academic and criminal records
2. Integrity: to prevent unauthorized modification of files and to maintain the status quo; including system, information and personal
3. Availability: to prevent unauthorized withholding of information from those who need it when they need it.

These three elements, and hence total security, can only be achieved through vigorous reinforcement of the three principles of security, namely protection, detection and reaction.

The object of an attack through unauthorized access, use and alteration is always a computer system. Computer systems have three components: hardware, software and humanware. Each one of these components is a target of attack. We therefore consider three types of security to cover these three components.

To prevent access, intrusion and alteration of a physical facility, a facility needs to have physical barriers that resist penetration from intruders. Such physical barriers may include fences, lock and key, and/or human and animal guards.

Software security is achieved through the use of a strong authentication system, an unbreakable encryption standard, application of audit trails, and a religiously frequent check of the software components. Encryption is intended to secure the privacy of information over the communication channels by keeping information hidden from unintended parties. Authentication on the other hand secures information in storage through a process of user identification, using passwords and other secure forms, like digital signatures.

The security of humanware depends on personal identity. Personal identity is made up of digitized physical characteristics together with assigned attributes, like identity numbers and names. Verification of personal identity, is done through authentication of physical characteristics and personal attributes, and failure to authenticate an individual means failure to authenticate personal identity which in the digital age is based on numbers like social security, driver's license, telephone and fax numbers and e-mail address. Although digital authentication is easy, it is more often compromised because of these numbers being stored in huge databases where security cannot be 100 percent guaranteed.

There will never be a totally secure computer system because the security of a system depends on the intertwined security of its three basic components of hardware, software and humanware, yet no one can guarantee 100 percent security of any one component of the system. Hence the only known secure system is one that has no contact with the outside world, no modern connections, no network connection and is completely closed in a bunker, but such a system would be useless.

Pseudosecurity can be provided to systems through a policy commonly known as "security through obscurity" (STO). The use of STO tends to create a belief that the system can be secure as long as there is no knowledge passed to those outside the system concerning the internal function of the system, but it assumes that nobody outside the system will ever find out. Military organizations always try to implement these types of pseudosecurity systems. Pseudosecurity of course depends on a small band of trusted workers, assuming that none leaves or retire from the establishment. But people move and people retire, so the assumption and hopes of pseudosecurity are not realistic.

Protection

Protection of system security, including individual security, depends on a thorough knowledge of the system, including knowledge of what

constitutes security for the system in question and what the security requirements are. Once security requirements are known, then the next step
would be an evaluation of those requirements, sorting out the basic ones
and prioritizing them. With priorities in place, then a search for security
mechanisms to implement the list follows. Such mechanisms or techniques
must be evaluated to make sure that they will be effective or satisfactory
when employed, so at this stage an effective method of implementation must
be sought. Among the current security mechanisms of choice is cryptography. In fact cryptography has so far proved to be the best technique to
guarantee information security. It prevents fraud, provides accountability
and accuracy needed in electronic transmission, assures validity in electronic commerce, protects anonymity and also authenticates individual
identity. But although cryptography is praised as good, it should not be
taken as the wonder security technique. According to Bruce Schneir, cryptography can withstand targeted attacks up to a point, but it is easy to get
the sought information using some other ways (19). In fact, cryptography
does not prevent every electronic security breach, especially those taking
place offline like the security of operating systems.

Detection

The implementation of security mechanisms cannot assure total system security. In fact, as any security expert would say, it is naive to expect
total system security. Good security techniques always assume that there
will be attempts, from either within the system or outside it, to breach the
established security mechanism. Because, no one can be totally sure of a
full protection mechanism, our second focus should be the ability to detect
security breaches and foil them. The detection mechanism should be used
by system managers to better understand the infrastructure in the security of the system and to work within it to constantly monitor the system
for interference. In addition, the detection mechanism should include a
good and regularly varied monitoring system to enhance security techniques
already in place. Security monitoring is crucial to the overall security of
the system because of the rapidly changing technology that renders security systems obsolete in a very short time and usually without security
experts knowing it. In fact a security expert is like a spy constantly review-
ing every new security technology in comparison with what one has, which
makes keeping abreast of security technology a very daunting job.

Reaction

It is always a good security technique to assume that however good the security program in place is, sooner or later there will be a security breach. And when such a breach occurs, there are contingent plans to contain it through a clearly defined recovery plan. Such a plan should include the detection and determination of the security holes, a way to plug the holes created, a program to enhance the security around the system to deter other intruders from using the same techniques, and a plan to identify the intruders and hopefully prosecute them. This damage control plan must be thorough and very well executed because security attacks once they occur, usually destroy in a few hours the security and users' confidence in the system, which can take years to rebuild. The plan should include mechanisms to rebuild the lost confidence in the shortest time possible.

Censorship

No issue raises more heated and sometimes spirited debate than the issue of Internet censorship. In fact, many in the public have come to learn of the Internet through these debates and the corresponding news coverage. To make sure that we do not lose the focus of this discussion ourselves, we will examine online censorship, which is, broadly speaking, an attempt to restrict access to the Internet and its content by an established authority. The debate about online censorship and its sister issue, online access, pits two determined and uncompromising groups against each other: those advocating some degree of Internet censorship to curb Internet indecent material and hate speech and the democratic crusaders who think of any Internet censorship as an up-front attack on free speech and hence an attack on the institutions of democratic societies and international law. As a powerful new medium, the Internet consists of a multiplicity of systems that incorporate older media like print, broadcast and transmission each with its individual characteristics. However, unlike older media, Internet media are more versatile because of the speed and domain of coverage. For example, communication is both one-to-one and one-to-many and is very fast and global in nature, with no physical and jurisdiction barriers.

To the pro-censorship camp, these Internet characteristics — the ability to hide one's identity, the inability of individuals to remove offensive materials at will, and the ease of getting to these materials — have all made the traditionally enshrined issue of free speech too free on the Internet. They believe that the Internet has reached a point where free speech is creating a potential danger to children. Concerned parents and the religious right, the two groups most noticeable in this camp, believe that children need to be protected from violence, sexually explicit materials and abuse. Although children have become the focal point of the rallying cry, there are other issues like defamation, hate speech and the distribution of free how-to manuals for crimes.

Just as spirited is the other camp, the so-called champions of democracy, freedom, human rights and free speech. They believe that the protection of free speech overrides all other human concerns. This group, comprises mostly seasoned Internet users, human rights activists and other free-spirited 60s-like individuals. To them, those who call for any form of censorship are ignorant of the Internet culture. They are techno-illiterates and fear their children, who are usually more computer literate than they. Whatever argument the anti-censorship camp gives, there is a growing awareness in all sectors of society and in almost every country that something, however small, has to be done. This realization has prompted governments around the world to try to protect their children, stop terrorists, silence racists and protect national security. This kind of protection is done in a number of ways, including censorship and limitation to Internet access. Those denying access do so either to an entire segment of their populations through exorbitant charges or by confining access to limited sectors of society. In Chapter Five we will discuss these efforts in detail.

Information Overload and Health

The growth of the Internet has created an unprecedented explosion of information. Every minute we are bombarded with exponentially increasing amounts of information from the Internet, e-mail, voice mail, television, radio, newspapers, magazines, news features and local networks. The search for the right information from this mountain of information has become more complex, overwhelming our capacity to cope, analyze, synthesize and disseminate that information. The decision-making process depends on information one has but, more important on the organization of that information, which may involve combining various fragments of information from different sources. Good personal and business decisions depend heavily on good use of information available to the decisionmaker. In the information age, where there is an information overload, the capacity to make an effective decision may be impaired and may lead to economic losses unless there is good information management. Good information management is affected by the source, the amount and the nature of information. According to Hal Berghel, all the following Internet factors affect information management (20):

1. Internet Credibility

    The Web on the Internet doubles as a private and public information and communication medium. In both of these capacities the Web takes in personal Webpages as well as public information. The result is that the Web content, hence Internet content, does not guarantee accuracy, value or utility, hence no guaranteed credibility.

2. Nature of Search Engines

    The search engines started as well-intentioned tools to index the wealth of information and consequently help the user in the search. However, search engines, in an effort to boost their index bases, index more junk than anything else, causing any search to result in hundreds of thousands of hits, 90 percent of which is junk.

    Many Internet users try to employ a helping hand from personal information agents, which are software programs that act on behalf of the user to organize and index information. Personal information agents use a number of techniques:

    (a) semiautonomous agents to whom a user delegates the tasks of information management

    (b) knowledge based intelligent agents that have adopted capacity so that the agent can at times use this knowledge base to adopt techniques that suit the situation and type of information. An example of such intelligent agents is UCEgo, a Unix-based agent that can do planning, provide information and make corrections of user misconceptions for users of Unix operating systems. There are also agents for electronic mail handling, meeting scheduling, electronic news filtering, and agents to recommend books, music and other forms of entertainment. However, there is still lack of trust and competency problems associated with these agents.

3. Lack of Internet Brand and Brand Loyalty

    The value and credibility of information on the Internet would be greatly increased if there were a way to review, classify and rank the information. Such mechanisms would help individuals and companies develop brands, and customers would look for brand names and eventually adhere to brand loyalty the way they do with other brand products. Second to information overload is individual health, what psychologists now refer to as Information Fatigue Syndrome. According to psychologist David Lewis, quoted in Kathy Nellis, "We're often seeing a failure of concentration. We are seeing a loss of motivation, loss of morale. We are seeing greater irritability." (21)

However, Information Fatigue Syndrome is not mental. In a survey conducted in five countries — Britain, the United States, China (Hong Kong), Singapore, and Australia — results show that the main complaint is stress (21). According to Lewis, the stress may cause digestive disorders and other effects on personal and sex lives. Other ills related to the Internet fall into the traditional category of Repetitive Strain Injury (RSI), which is a set of work-related musculoskeletal disorders caused by repeated and prolonged body movement, resulting in damage to the fiber and soft tissues like tendons, nerves and muscles.

Chapter 4

The Internet as Global Media: Regulation and Control Tools

By its very nature the Internet falls within three different media. First, it acts as a communication medium by its e-mail facilities. Second, it can be considered a computer services medium because it is a meganetwork of computer networks. And third, it acts as a broadcast service, much like television, radio and newspapers, because of its capacity to carry news and information.

Each one of these three media presents unique problems. For example, as a communication medium, the Internet presents all the problems of information security in databases, at servers and during transmission, and all issues of eavesdropping and wiretapping do arise. As a computer service, it presents system security problems, both hardware and software, and as a broadcast medium, it inherits all traditional problems of broadcast media that serve diverse audiences and the realization that it is difficult to please everyone all the time. The value and utility of the Internet as global media then depend on what medium one is in and the value of the content one gets out. For example, the value one attaches to the Internet as a broadcast medium does not apply in the computer services medium. This means that the perceptions, expectations and concerns are different in each medium. As a computer services medium, for example, Internet dangers are more in computer networks and software security, areas that do not concern a lot of everyday people except a few network managers and engineers and software developers.

However, when considered as a communication medium, the Internet reveals a lot of new issues of concern involving a lot of people. Most notable among these issues is content value. Content value depends of course on the security of information both during storage and transmission. The number of everyday people affected by information security is big, and information security concerns are on every CEO's mind. And finally as a broadcast medium, the Internet becomes a billboard, a newspaper, a television, a radio, a newsmagazine and everything in between. It therefore becomes a carrier of everything good and bad that all these media have carried before it. However, the Internet carries all these things faster, better, more efficiently and cheaper, while covering a lot more ground and exhibiting an unprecedented ease of access.

As we pointed out earlier, broadcast media have the most problems with the general public because it is extremely difficult to please everyone in the diverse cultural, religious, linguistic, educational and geographical global population. So our focus in this chapter is on the Internet as a communication medium and as a broadcast medium, with special emphasis on the latter because its problems are more diverse and most controversial.

The Internet as a Communication Medium: Security and Control Mechanisms

As a communication medium the Internet's fundamental problem is security of information in storage in large databases on the Internet servers and during transmission between source and sink. The Internet's ability to globally bring these databases into the reach of individual computers created a potential for any computer user to access any of these databases at will. With a lot of individual, business, military and national information in these databases, information security in storage and during transmission has become the greatest concern to individuals, military strategists, business executives and national security experts. Not so long ago system security concerns were the privilege of computer system managers, but now they concern every computer user. In fact the fear of system security breakdown through intrusion is high not only among computer system managers and individual users but also among company executives, military planners and government officials. In the United States, for example, according to Robert Marsh, head of the President's Commission on Critical Infrastructure Protection, "The United States lacks the tools to fight a possible computer assault on critical infrastructure." This fear has made the information-attack issue one of the top national security issues (1). According to John Deutch, CIA director, the threat to the nation of a cyberspace attack as compared to the dangers posed by nuclear, chemical and biological weapons "is very, very close to the top" (2). This fear is probably also true with corporate America infrastructures, although no studies have been done; however, with the business community, the fear of system security breakdown is understandable because since the end of the cold war, all international military and strategic espionage shifted ground; it is now industrial espionage, and according to Keith Rhodes of the General Accounting Office, "every node [on the Internet] is a potential spy" (3). As we saw in Chapter Three, the security of information does not only depend on the security of information on computer systems acting as network servers, although this forms a bigger part of the security concerns. It also depends on weaknesses in network software like Internet browsers, operating systems and every network application software stored on servers.

Besides the security of information at servers and on network computers, another area of information security concerns is information transmission, where through eavesdropping, information security can be compromised. With such a threat of unsecured transmission lines, all types of future business, strategic and private communications are at risk. Yet electronic commerce is predicted to become one of the fastest and largest components of the Internet within the coming years. Security controls to be considered need to cover server security, server access and transmission. This will involve both hardware and software controls because of the complementary role of software in Internet communication and broadcasting. Software security will involve operating system security, both stand-alone and network, and information management.

Hardware System Security and Control

Hardware security controls are varied and involve access to hardware resources like memory and files, authentication routines for file access, password protection and the use of firewalls. These controls are divided into six areas:

1. Prevention

    This is intended to restrict access to information on the system by preventing access to a server on a network. The prevention is achieved through such technologies as will permit only authorized people to the designated areas. Such technologies include, for example, firewalls.

2. Protection

    This is intended to identify all security requirements of the system, evaluating them and coming up with the most suitable and most comprehensive techniques, which are then deployed to protect the system.

3. Detection

    Detection is intended to provide early warning for discovery of security breaches that have bypassed both protection and prevention mechanisms. It should, therefore, use a monitoring program, which should be updated continuously and consistently.

4. Limitation

    This mechanism is intended to cut the losses suffered in case of failed security. It could come in different forms to fit the situation. One form could be a public relations blitz while in other forms it could be high-tech recovery systems.

5. Reaction

    This involves the analysis of the security lapses, the type of lapses and the efforts to come up with remedies for a better security system based on the failures observed.

6. Recovery

    Finally this is intended to recover as efficiently as possible what has been lost and update contingent recovery plans for the system in case of future failures.

Firewalls

The security of information on a network client computer depends partly on the physical security of that computer to deter unauthorized access and partly to the security of the network that the computer is connected to. If that network, be it company or institutional, is connected to the Internet, then the security of the client computer also depends on the security of the Internet as a whole, which many believe is not secure at all. Networks with insecure connections to the Internet are very vulnerable to external

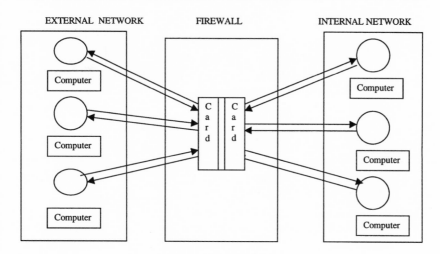

Figure 4.1: Firewall

attack. How then can the security of a network connected to the Internet be achieved? The answer is a *firewall*. A firewall is a computer with two Ethernet cards connecting two networks, as shown in Figure 4.1 above. One network on one card is an internal and secure network, and the other network on the second card is a nonsecure external network.

The machine is then set up to accept, deny or pass network traffic in both directions. Only authorized traffic is allowed to pass through these bottleneck security barriers. Firewalls have two benefits. First they allow the control and monitoring of network traffic by the network manager of the local network, and they simplify and localize the security problems of a local network on a single device, thus making security management easy.

Firewalls as network security techniques are becoming very popular, especially as the issues of Internet security become more complicated and publicized. There are basically two types of firewalls:

Packet Filter. A *packet filter* is a multilevel firewall that compares every packet of data going through it to a set of its traffic rules, checking information in the packet like source and destination addresses, types of services requested and the type of communication service used. The packet is then denied or accepted for passage through the pathways. But because of this overhead, the use of packet filters is limited.

Proxy Server. A *proxy server* firewall provides a higher-level filtering than packet filters by examining the traffic streams as a connection to a

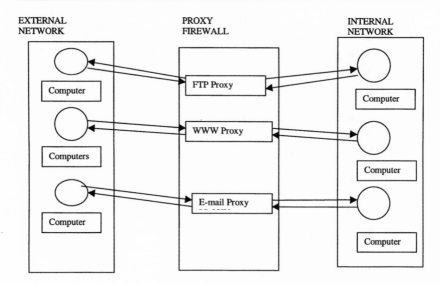

Figure 4.2: Proxy Servers

network service. Unlike filters, however, proxy servers are more flexible and can provide many more additional security functions like user-level authentication, end-to-end encryption data, intelligent logging, information hiding and access restriction based on service types. Rather than examining each packet that flows through it like a filter firewall, a proxy server firewall starts a new proxy for each new communication session to handle such an application. For example, if a client wants to send an e-mail, the client computer network sends the mail to the local network, which forwards it to the proxy server; the server then creates an e-mail proxy to authenticate the mail. If it is accepted the e-mail is then forwarded to the external network, and the proxy is killed. Each proxy handles one application. This means that there may be many similar applications with different proxies running at the same time. See Figure 4.2 above.

The creation of a proxy for every application offers the following advantages (Softway http:/www.softway.com.au/softway/firewalls/parta.html):

1. prevention of exploitation of security loopholes in the network it is protecting,
2. higher-level filtering and more focused and specific security,
3. ease of maintainability and configuration,
4. better traceability because of good audit and centralized control.

Although firewall security mechanisms are hailed as good because firewalls can isolate the local networks from other networks, not all types of firewalls are equal in security. In fact proxy server firewalls are thought to offer the most security, whereas packet filter firewalls offer better performance.

Internet Transmission Security

Many have likened the Internet to a global network of highways connecting millions of cities. Packets of information, using TCP/IP protocol suites, move from one server to another, as do cars and trucks from one city to another. Information moves on electronic highways between servers, in the same way cars and trucks move goods between cities, following a protocol. The security of the goods moved on the highways can also be likened to the security of information on the Internet. On highways, highway robbers attack cars and/or trucks and steal their contents as do Internet eavesdroppers, who can tap into a transmission channel and steal information. One way to stop highway robbery is to secure the highways. There are many ways of doing this. One method may involve the locking of cars and trucks during transmission so that highway robbers, even if they get hold of the trucks, cannot open them because they do not have keys. In a similar manner, those transmitting information on the Internet can use a secure scheme commonly known as *cryptography* or secure writing.

Cryptography. Cryptography, according to Karen Forchet, is the art and science of secret communication, embracing all kinds of communications including codes and signaling (2). The security of communication in cryptography is achieved through the use of mathematical and logical functions that transform data into unintelligible forms, a process known as encryption, before transmission and back into intelligible forms, a process known as decryption, after the transmission.

In communication, especially modern digital communication, cryptography is a vital part of information security policy. It provides the needed lock and key to information handling on the Internet. The security provided by cryptography then enables individuals and businesses to protect their sensitive information during transmission and in files in databases. Internet commerce is expected to grow almost exponentially as better Internet technology develops. This growth, and indeed the growth of the entire Internet, will depend on the security of sensitive information while on the Internet, hence on cryptography. According to William Murray, cryptography provides us with the means to create unforgeable signatures, issue credentials, exchange electronic money, authenticate a speaker or sender and speak in private (4). Digital communication and commerce need electronic envelopes and digital signatures, which are provided by cryptography.

Data Encryption and Decryption. An original message from the sender is called *plaintext*, and the encrypted message to the receiver is called a *ciphertext*. In order for anyone, including the recipient, to recover a ciphertext, they must use a key. There are three commonly used key systems: a private key or symmetric key system as it is sometimes called, in which only one key is used; a public key or asymmetric key system in which two keys are used, consisting of both private and public keys; a one-time pad system in which the key can be as long as the message and there are no restrictions on a key.

Data encryption and decryption transform intelligible plaintext to be transferred into unintelligible ciphertext before it is transmitted and then recover the data in its original intelligible form on arrival. This process prevents third parties from interfering with the data, ensuring privacy by keeping the data inaccessible to anybody without authorization, just like in the case of the cars and trucks on highways.

At the receiving end of the message, the recipient is assured of the identity of the sender and the integrity of the message by a protocol called authentication. In our modern-day digital age, the authentication protocol involves a digital signature very similar to the handwritten signature. The digital signature is an unforgeable piece of data asserting that the named person wrote or agreed to the message. A secure digital signature consists of two parts: a method of signing the message that is unforgeable and a method of verifying that the signature was by the person whom it represents.

Authentication protocols are based on either public-key or secret-key cryptosystems. The secret-key cryptosystem allows the sender to use the key to encrypt the message, and the receiver of the message uses the same secret key to decrypt the message. The problem with secret-key cryptosystems is getting the two parties to agree on the secret key in total secrecy.

In public-key cryptosystems on the other hand, each person gets a pair of keys, called public and private keys. Each party's public key is published, but the private key remains secret. The transmitted data is encrypted using a public key, but it can only be decrypted using a private key. No keys are passed between the sender and receiver of the message. Public-key cryptosystems are used in both encryption and authentication. In encryption anybody who wants to send you a message looks up your public key, uses it to encrypt your message and transmits it. Upon receipt of the message you use your private key to decrypt the message. In authentication the sender uses a private key together with the message and passes them through a computation whose output is the signature. The signature is then attached to the encrypted message. The receiver of the message and digital signature does another computation involving the message, the signature and the sender's public key. Digital signatures are difficult to forge once signed and are difficult to disown.

There are a number of cryptosystems in use today including the following:

1. RSA is a public-key cryptosystem for both encryption and authentication invented in 1977 by Ron Rivest and Adi Shamir. It generates both the public and private keys from a pair of large prime numbers through a series of computations. Let P0 be a public key, S0 a private key and M a plaintext. Suppose sender X wants to send message M to Y; X encrypts the message as P0(M) and Y recovers the meaningful message M as S0(P0(M))= M. Similarly Y can send the message to X.

2. Data Encryption Standards (DES) is an encryption block cipher developed at IBM. It is a secret-key cryptosystem that involves only one secret key, which must be known by both the sender and receiver. It operates on a 64-bit block of data with a 56-bit key, and it is embedded in hardware; hence it is fast.

3. Clipper Chip is an encryption chip developed by the U.S. government as part of the Capstone Project, a four-part set of standards for publicly available cryptology. The four parts of the Capstone Project include a bulk-data-encryption algorithm, a digital-signature algorithm, a key-exchange protocol, and a hash function. The clipper chip is the bulk-data-encryption algorithm commonly known as Skipjack (5). The Clipper was developed to balance the needs for private secure communication with those of government law enforcement agencies to gain access to communications of suspected criminals. The Clipper balances those opposing needs through a key escrow, a process whereby keys are kept by an additional third party who can make them available to law enforcement agencies through court authorization. As expected, the Clipper Chip has been very controversial, primarily because of the escrow keys.

4. Digital Signature Standards (DSS) is a U.S. government–proposed public-key digital-signature standard. It is one of the four parts of the Capstone Project. It is an authentication standard that uses a discrete log problem based on the work of Schnorr and El Gamal (6). Although DSS has some benefits over its rival the RSA, it has been shrouded in controversy over its lack of key-exchange capabilities, its slow speed in verification of signatures, its incompatibility with existing international standards (like ISO, CCITT and SWIFT) and the fact that the Internet has for long been used to RSA (6). DSS works by using a pair of public and private keys to generate and verify a digital signature. The keys are used together with a hash function. For example, one who holds a private key may generate a signature for data, and the holder of the public key then verifies the signature. Anybody who does not know the private key cannot generate a verifiable signature.

5. PEMS is an Internet Privacy Enhanced Mail Standard designed and supported by the Internet Activities Board to provide secure electronic mail. It includes encryption, authentication and key management, but it supports only a few cryptographic algorithms (5).

6. IDEA is a symmetric key cryptographic software with a 128-bit key. It works by using one key to encrypt and decrypt the message. For example, if X wants to send message M to recipient Y, then X encrypts this message M as $IDEA(X,K)$. Y receives this gibberish message, and he or she applies the key again as $IDEA(IDEA(X,K))$ = M.

7. MD5 is another cryptographic software with 128-bit one-way hash on inputs. Without the hash function, it is usually impossible to determine the inputs.

8. RIPEM is another program that offers security of Internet e-mail. It provides encryption and digital signatures using RSA and DES routines (5).

9. Public Key Cryptography Standards (PKCS) is a standard that implements public-key cryptography and is compatible with a number of standards like ISO, PEM and ITT (5).

10. Pretty Good Privacy (PGP)—is a powerful cryptographic software for mostly low computers running MS-DOS, UNIX and VAX/VMS. It comprises three components: RSA, *IDEA,* and MD5 discussed above. PGP is used in encryption, decryption, signing and authentication (7).

The history of encryption is as old as humanity itself. Emperors, kings, governments, lovers and almost any two parties have been using some form of encryption for generations. Encryption can be done in one of two ways: substitution or transposition. *Substitution* is a process that involves substituting one unit of the ciphertext with a comparable unit of the plaintext(s). The substituted unit may be one or more characters. *Transposition* is a process involving moving around one or more units of the plaintext within the text documents. Encrypting or decrypting a text using either of these two schemes follows a regimen of rules called an encryption algorithm.

Software Security Controls

Besides the hardware controls discussed in the previous section, which have more local flavors, there are also software tools again displaying more local and individual controls of the security of Internet information. However, on the Internet, with its reflection of the real world and its ability to transcend national barriers, comprehensive control tools are difficult if not impossible to apply due to the global mosaic of jurisdiction, culture, religion and political interests. So the tools, mostly software, that have local and individual control initiatives are more appealing because they give each individual user personal control, and they are not as technical as the hardware controls we have seen before. Such tools include client and network operating systems and Internet server and browser software.

Operating System Software

As computers become a common fixture in our daily lives and as bigger and bigger computer networks get formed, the old questions are still being asked but with louder voices and in unison: Can people really rely on computers to store their vital data? Who can access certain computer resources? Can people be prevented from accessing resources they are not authorized to access? Answers to these questions are probably found in both stand-alone and network operating systems.

An operating system (OS) is a set of core programs that together manage the resources of a computer system or network. It is an interface between the hardware and the user application programs. Because an operating system is a set of programs, designing it is a complex task. It is a known fact in programming circles that the more complex a program design is, the higher the potential for errors. Hence operating systems have a higher potential for security-related problems. Most errors occur during design due to poor design specifications or during system implementation, generation, maintenance and modification. Other potential areas where flaws are likely to be introduced include input/output, ambiguity in access policy, incomplete modification, and authorization of tasks and lack of standardized procedures. The security of an operating system depends on the security of the kernel, the operating system part that is at the lowest level of functionality responsible for synchronization, interprocess communication, message passing and interrupt handling. And the security of information on a computer system depends on the operating system used because the operating system is the interface, the gateway between the user and the hardware. So in order to uphold the security of information, security controls in an operating system must be enforced. Such controls may include the following:

1. User identification and authentication that requires users to have a password for authentication and to log on the system for identification every time they want to use it

2. Authentication procedures that set clear and precise procedures stating each user's possible access rights, limitations, what needs to be done to acquire other access rights, and a good monitoring system to check on the performance of these procedures

3. File protection mechanism that monitors and strictly regulates access to system files. Such a mechanism may include labeling all files, indicating type of information contained and the security level of the files, generating a restriction list indicating the type of restriction on each file, and identifying the resources needed to keep these controls in place

4. System protection that sets up protection controls that may include lock and key, installation of security gadgets to limit the number of attempts during logons, shutting down the system and offline terminals if not in use and encouraging users to safeguard and periodically change their passwords.

Network Operating System Security. Operating system security issues also extend to network operating systems or distributed operating systems. Distributed computing can be defined loosely as a collaboration involving a number of computers on a network working together to accomplish a task. The security challenges presented by distributed operating systems include the need to be able to integrate and synchronize individual systems' security technologies such as authentication, access control and cryptology. Special care must be taken in dealing with this integration of policies to promote a smooth interoperability of all security policies in the network.

Another tool that has been used by network operating systems to enhance security is network *enclaves*. An enclave is a group of computers around which a security parameter is maintained with much stronger defenses around the perimeter than those inside the enclave. Enclave security technology may include firewalls. However, when enclosure techniques are used, efforts must be made to ensure trust among users.

Security Information Management

As operating systems' uses increase and the number of different operating systems' technologies and the sizes and types of network increase, security issues become more complex. Different security mechanisms and protocols are being developed every day, and keeping up with that stream of new techniques and methods is becoming increasingly difficult.

The problem is even more complex in distributed computing, where each site may have customized and specialized techniques and protocols. So a management scheme is necessary to effectively synchronize these differing mechanisms and protocols and to protect the system from unauthorized accesses by those taking advantage of weak points and loopholes resulting from the integration.

Server and Browser Software Security

The problems of server and browser software security fall within the general problem area of security. As in general software, server and browser software errors result from programming and data bugs. Recent reports of gaping holes in both of the world's leading browsers — Netscape Navigator 4.0 and Microsoft Explorer 3.0 — highlighted the vulnerability of Internet users. In Netscape's case, the hole was found by a small Dutch software company. The bug could allow Web-site operators to read anything stored on a hard disk of any PC logged on the Web site.

A similar security breach was found in Microsoft Windows 95 and Windows NT Internet Explorer 3.0 and 3.01. The bug allows hackers to use .LNK and .URL files to access programs on a remote computer without the owner of the computer knowing about it. Hackers could even launch their own programs like a Trojan virus onto your computer.

Together Microsoft and Netscape Internet browsers control about 90 percent of the world's browser market, and errors like these are not very reassuring for those who need security on the Internet. Internet security trapdoors are not only limited to Internet browsers but are also in Internet software, especially server software like Fast Track from Netscape, Mail Server, Proxy Server, Enterprise Server, News Server and Catalog Server. Besides Web browsers and server software, Internet security loopholes are also found in Network technologies like ActiveX, a Microsoft Internet technology, and Java applets, a Sun Microsystems technology developed to protect the browsers. The weaknesses in Internet software technology were demonstrated by an embarrassing incident on German television when the Chaos Computer Club, a German hacker group from Hamburg, demonstrated on a television show to a national audience how they could use Microsoft ActiveX technology to steal money from one account over the Internet and move it into another account by bypassing control requirements like the Personal Identification Number (PIN).

Although Java is a more secure technology than ActiveX, the problem still remains. The tools to fight browser bugs have been ad hoc and haphazard, with both Netscape and Microsoft only responding to reported bugs by offering plugs. However, on technology security, Microsoft has responded by putting Authenticode in its Explorer 3.0. Authenticode tries to identify who published the executable code the user is downloading from the Internet; then the user can make a quick decision (the browser informs the user that what he or she is about to use is an unsigned code). It also verifies that the code has not been altered since first publication. Both Sun Microsystems and Netscape have also started to include code signing, following Microsoft's lead.

The Internet as a Broadcast Medium: Security and Control Mechanisms

Broadcast media controversies are not new. Since the beginning of the print medium, the first component of the broadcast media, controversies involving burning of printed materials, imprisonment of authors and journalists and many times death to news media personnel have all been common practice. The Internet, with its new interfaces to the old print, video and audio media, together with its other added characteristics, has inherited all the broadcast media ills and controversies. These controversies all center around media content.

Historically the broadcast media have never come to terms with their audiences on the question of content. This results from the fact that the media serve a diverse audience, a mosaic of differing cultural, religious, educational, geographical and political interests. The Internet, because it has combined all known broadcast media in one, has gotten a full and free share of all these controversies. Evidently the Internet audience has fractured into interest camps. Most prominent of these camps are the two opposing groups, one seeking Internet content control and the other ostensibly opposed to any form of Internet control. There seems to be little room for compromise between these two groups because any form of restriction on the Internet is likely to be seen as too restrictive by one group and too permissive by the other.

When one looks critically at these controversies, one immediately notices that the underlying problem common to them is Internet access. Parents, teachers, religious leaders and concerned individuals are in general all seeking for controls to be put on Internet access, and they are all talking about who should have access to the Internet and what constitutes acceptable Internet content. So let us start our discussion with this in mind.

Access to Internet Content

As we saw in the previous chapter, for many ordinary folks, what propelled the success of the Internet — easy and mass access to Internet content — is the same thing that is causing the greatest security and privacy concerns. The issue of easy access to pornographic and other indecent materials, for example, has been a lightning rod to calls for censorship of the Internet by one camp and a rallying cry to protect the free speech, human rights and constitutional rights by those opposed to Internet censorship.

In fact, for a majority of ordinary people with a home computer, the issues of computer system security, eavesdropping, servers security and all related information security matters and individual privacy are of little concern. What concerns them most and constantly concerns the politicians who get their votes is the fear of their children getting easy access to indecent and objectionable materials, their unfriendly neighbor and coworker getting the how-to manual for bomb making, and Aunt Ruth getting hate mail and speeches. These are the Internet issues that the public want their governments to address; the technocrats can worry about everything else.

Our aim in this section is to give a survey of available control tools for those who want to use them. We have divided our findings into the following categories: legislative, self-regulatory, mass education, advocacy and hot lines.

Legislative Initiatives

As the debate between freedom-of-speech advocates and those more concerned with the protection of children heats up, the political fallout is resulting in governments around the world revising current policies, charters and acts and legislating new ones. As we will see in detail in the next section, this has been one of the most popular, and to politicians the most visible, means of Internet control. Legislative efforts are backed by judicial and law enforcement machinery. In the United States, for example, in the last few years, a number of outdated acts have been rewritten to bring them up to date. The degree of effectiveness of this approach varies from country to country. In some countries it is approaching censorship, as is the case in both China and Singapore. In other countries, however, there have been minor changes to existing laws. Between these two extremes is an array of models.

Besides purely legislative processes, which are more public, there are also private initiatives that work either in conjunction with public judicial systems and law enforcement agencies or through workplace forces. Examples abound of large companies, especially high technology companies like software, telecommunications and Internet providers, coming together, either forming consortiums of some form or partnerships and devising implementable control techniques.

Self-Regulation

Even though the debate for control has been heated and sometimes plain ugly, some governments in a number of countries and regional groupings have resisted introducing new laws targeting the Internet. The argument, which at least for the time being seems to be working in a number of countries, is that current laws, with minor changes to reflect the new technological reality and changes, are adequate. This line of thought is based on the fact that the Internet has not yet introduced any new crimes into the already-known crime repertoire. Consequently a number of countries are choosing to try, at least for the moment, the self-regulatory route, leaving individuals who make up the bulk of Internet users to find their own individual control tools to suit their liking and needs. In fact Internet software technology has developed to such an extent that the tools for personal control are already available and cheap. Even the U.S. government, in the wake of the Communication Decency Act (CDA) defeat, realized this when the White House organized the Internet/Online Summit to enhance law enforcement and educate the public on Internet safety and advocate a rating and labeling system for the Internet (8). The crusade for voluntarily self-regulating the Internet, using rating and labeling software, is led by industry giants Microsoft and America Online (9). The rating and labeling standards are based on a *PICS* technology. PICS stands for "Platform for Internet Content Selection," a mechanism for labeling Web pages according to their content based on a set of criteria developed by rating software firms. The labels attached to the Web pages are then used by the filtering software when the page is being accessed.

Platform for Internet Content Selection (PICS). PICS, Platform for Internet Content Selection, a cross-industry working group with a mission to facilitate the development of technologies that give Internet users and any other interactive medium control of the content they see as offensive, established label formats that attach ratings to Web pages and distribution methods without directly dictating the vocabulary to the user or who should use what, leaving the user software to interpret the content and make a decision whether to block access or verify the content's integrity before granting access. This means that any group or individual can come up with their own standards for accepting or rejecting Web pages and then apply the PICS technology to create their own database by using a PICS generator. The resulting META data from the generator is added to the document header as shown below:

```
<HTML>
<HEAD><TITLE> Title-name</TITLE>
<META http-equiv ="PICS-Label" content='(PICS labels here....)'>
</HEAD>
.

.
</HTML>
```

It is also possible to apply PICS technology to non–HTML documents. Already a number of individuals, Webmasters, browser developers like

Microsoft (in Internet Explorer [IE]) and search sites like AltaVista are using the technology.

Rating and Labeling. Rating of Internet content is very similar to the rating of movies and videos, and it follows a similar procedure, resulting in an assigned label. There are a number of rating companies, most of whom support PICS technology and standards. The two most notable of these are *RASC* and *SafeSurf.*

RSAC or RSACi rating system is open and content based, providing blocking capabilities for entire sites, sections or even individual pages or files within a site. Its rating process goes through four steps (10):

1. The Webmaster selects the granularity or scope of the item being rated.
2. A one-page questionnaire requesting demographic information is completed and used to authenticate the address of the Web site being rated.
3. Four questions in each of the four content areas of *Sex, Nudity, Language* and *Violence* and a checklist of very specific terms about how the content is portrayed are completed to determine the level and to generate a label for each content area.
4. At the end of the rating process, the score in each of the four content categories, the PICS meta tag to go into the header of the Web site, and detailed instructions about how to do this are all displayed on the screen and also sent to the rater by an e-mail message.

The RSAC rating system has about 20 category restrictions grouped into four descriptors of *Violence, Nudity, Sex* and *Language* and four levels as shown on the following page in Figure 4.3.*

The rating labels from the PICS generator should appear in the META label in the document HEAD in the PICS format as:

```
<HTML>
<HEAD>
<TITLE> This is a sample RSAC Rating System </TITLE>
<META http-equiv = "PICS-Label" content='PICS-1.1
"http://www.rsac.org/ratings" (rsac ratings here)'>
</HEAD>
    .

    .
</HTML>
```

RSAC Category Restriction menu was used by permission from RSAC.

	Violence Rating Descriptor	**Nudity Rating Descriptor**	**Sex Rating Descriptor**	**Language Rating Descriptor**
Level 4	Rape or wanton, Gratuitous violence	Frontal nudity (qualifying as provocative display)	Explicit sexual acts Or sex crimes	Crude, vulgar Language or extreme Hate speech
Level 3	Aggressive Violence or death To humans	Frontal nudity	Non-explicit sexual acts	Strong language or hate speech
Level 2	Destruction of realistic objects	Partial nudity	Clothed sexual touching	Moderate expletives or profanity
Level 1	Injury to human beings	Revealing attire	Passionate kissing	Mild expletives
Level 0	None of the above or sports related	None of the above	None of the above or innocent kissing romance	None of the above

Figure 4.3 RSACi Category Restriction Menu

SafeSurf is a rating, classification and filtering system using PICS technology and standards. SafeSurf's identification make is the SS~~ called the wave. The rating label from the PICS generator should appear in the META label in the document HEAD in the PICS format as:

```
<HTML>
<HEAD>
<TITLE> This is a sample SafeSurf Rating System </TITLE>
<META http-equiv = "PICS-Label" content='PICS-1.1
"http://www.classify.org/safesurf/" 1 r (SS~~ 000 1)'>
</HEAD>
.

.

</HTML>
```

SafeSurf has close to 90 category restrictions in its rating repertoire, grouped into ten SS~~ classification marks from SS~~000 to SS~~ 009, with each classification mark having close to nine levels as shown below.*

Section One: Adult Themes with Caution Levels

1. Profanity
   1) Subtle Innuendo
      description: Subtly implied through the use of slang

SafeSurf Category Restrictions are used by permission from SafeSurf.

2) Explicit Innuendo

   description: Explicitly implied through the use of slang

3) Technical Reference

   description: Dictionary, encyclopedic, news, technical references

4) Non-Graphic-Artistic

   description: Limited non-sexual expletives used in an artistic fashion

5) Graphic-Artistic

   description: Non-sexual expletives used in an artistic fashion

6) Graphic

   description: Limited use of expletives and obscene gestures

7) Detailed Graphic

   description: Casual use of expletives and obscene gestures

8) Explicit Vulgarity

   description: Heavy use of vulgar language and obscene gestures. Unsupervised Chat Rooms.

9) Explicit and Crude

   description: Saturated with crude sexual references and gestures. Unsupervised Chat Rooms.

2. Heterosexual Themes

   1) Subtle Innuendo

      description: Subtly implied through the use of metaphor

   2) Explicit Innuendo

      description: Explicitly implied (not described) through the use of metaphor

   3) Technical Reference

      description: Dictionary, encyclopedic, news, medical references

   4) Non-Graphic-Artistic

      description: Limited metaphoric descriptions used in an artistic fashion

   5) Graphic-Artistic

      description: Metaphoric descriptions used in an artistic fashion

   6) Graphic

      description: Descriptions of intimate sexual acts

   7) Detailed Graphic

      description: Descriptions of intimate details of sexual acts

   8) Explicitly Graphic or Inviting Participation

      description: Explicit descriptions of intimate details of sexual acts designed to arouse. Inviting interactive sexual participation. Unsupervised Sexual Chat Rooms or Newsgroups.

9) Explicit and Crude or Explicitly Inviting Participation
   description: Profane graphic descriptions of intimate details of sexual acts designed to arouse. Inviting interactive sexual participation. Unsupervised Sexual Chat Rooms or Newsgroups.
3. Homosexual Themes
   1) Subtle Innuendo
      description: Subtly implied through the use of metaphor
   2) Explicit Innuendo
      description: Explicitly implied (not described) through the use of metaphor
   3) Technical Reference
      description: Dictionary, encyclopedic, news, medical references
   4) Non-Graphic-Artistic
      description: Limited metaphoric descriptions used in an artistic fashion
   5) Graphic-Artistic
      description: Metaphoric descriptions used in an artistic fashion
   6) Graphic
      description: Descriptions of intimate sexual acts
   7) Detailed Graphic
      description: Descriptions of intimate details of sexual acts
   8) Explicitly Graphic or Inviting Participation
      description: Explicit descriptions of intimate details of sexual acts designed to arouse. Inviting interactive sexual participation. Unsupervised Sexual Chat Rooms or Newsgroups.
   9) Explicit and Crude or Explicitly Inviting Participation
      description: Profane Graphic Descriptions of intimate details of sexual acts designed to arouse. Inviting interactive sexual participation. Unsupervised Sexual Chat Rooms or Newsgroups.
4. Nudity
   1) Subtle Innuendo
      description: Subtly implied through the use of composition, lighting, shaping, revealing clothing, etc.
   2) Explicit Innuendo
      description: Explicitly implied (not shown) through the use of composition, lighting, shaping or revealing clothing
   3) Technical Reference
      description: Dictionary, encyclopedic, news, medical references

    4) Non–Graphic–Artistic
       description: Classic works of art presented in public museums for
          family viewing
    5) Graphic–Artistic
       description: Artistically presented without full frontal nudity
    6) Graphic
       description: Artistically presented with frontal nudity
    7) Detailed Graphic
       description: Erotic frontal nudity
    8) Explicit Vulgarity
       description: Pornographic presentation
    9) Explicit and Crude
       description: Explicit pornographic presentation
5. Violence
    1) Subtle innuendo
    2) Explicit innuendo
    3) Technical reference
    4) Non-graphic-artistic
    5) Graphic-artistic
    6) Graphic
    7) Detailed graphic
    8) Inviting participation in graphic interactive format
    9) Encouraging personal participation, weapon making
6. Sex, Violence, and Profanity
(Use to cover three themes with a single rating.)
    1) Subtle innuendo
    2) Explicit innuendo
    3) Technical reference
    4) Non-graphic-artistic
    5) Graphic-artistic
    6) Graphic
    7) Detailed graphic
    8) Explicit vulgarity
    9) Explicit and crude
7. Intolerance of another's race, religion, gender or sexual orientation
    1) Subtle innuendo
    2) Explicit innuendo
    3) Technical reference
    4) Non-graphic-literary

    5) Graphic-literary
    6) Graphic discussions
    7) Endorsing hatred
    8) Endorsing violent or hateful action
    9) Advocating violent or hateful action
8. Glorifying drug use
    1) Subtle innuendo
    2) Explicit innuendo
    3) Technical reference
    4) Non-graphic-artistic
    5) Graphic-artistic
    6) Graphic
    7) Detailed graphic
    8) Simulated interactive participation
    9) Soliciting personal participation
9. Other Adult Themes
    1) Subtle innuendo
    2) Explicit innuendo
    3) Technical reference
    4) Non-graphic-artistic
    5) Graphic-artistic
    6) Graphic
    7) Detailed graphic
    8) Explicit vulgarity
    9) Explicit and crude
A. Gambling
    1) Subtle innuendo
    2) Explicit innuendo
    3) Technical discussion
    4) Non-graphic-artistic, Advertising
    5) Graphic-artistic, Advertising
    6) Simulated gambling
    7) Real life gambling without stakes
    8) Encouraging interactive real life participation with stakes
    9) Providing means with stakes

Besides the two heavyweights above, there are less-known but upcoming companies like *Specs for Kids* for example. *Specs for Kids* has 11 dimensions with 5 category restrictions per dimension. The dimensions are varied enough to include politics, advertising, religion and alternative lifestyles.

Before the content is labeled, it is rated against a set of criteria. The criteria used by different rating agencies vary widely. For example cyber-NOT, a Sun MicroSystems rating and blocking system package, uses the following 12 categories in its category restriction menu shown in Figure 4.4 (11).

1. Violence/Profanity:

   To include pictures or text that display acts of cruelty both physical or emotional against people or animals with the intention of hurting or inflicting pain. Such acts may be extensive use of obscene words, phrases, and profanity.

2. Partial Nudity:

   To include any graphic images descriptive or not exposing female breasts, and buttocks, and male buttocks except parts showing in swimsuits.

3. Full Nudity:

   To include all graphic images descriptive or otherwise exposing any part of human genitalia except in scholarly taste that include graphic images in museums and scholarly publications.

4. Sexual Acts:

   Any graphic images descriptive or not exposing anyone or anything involved in explicit sexual acts of any form.

5. Gross Depiction:

   To include any graphic images descriptive or otherwise that are crude, vulgar and grossly deficient in civility and behavior.

6. Intolerance:

   This includes works in any media advocating prejudice and discrimination against any race, color, national origin, religion, disability or handicap, gender or sexual orientation.

7. Satanic or Cult:

   Satanic materials include among others, all graphic images descriptive or otherwise that contain sublime messages that may lead to devil worship, an affinity for evil, or wickedness.

8. Drugs/Drug Culture:

   This may include any graphic images descriptive or not that advocate any form of illegal use of drugs for entertainment.

9. Militant/Extremist :

   This includes any graphic images in any form that advocate

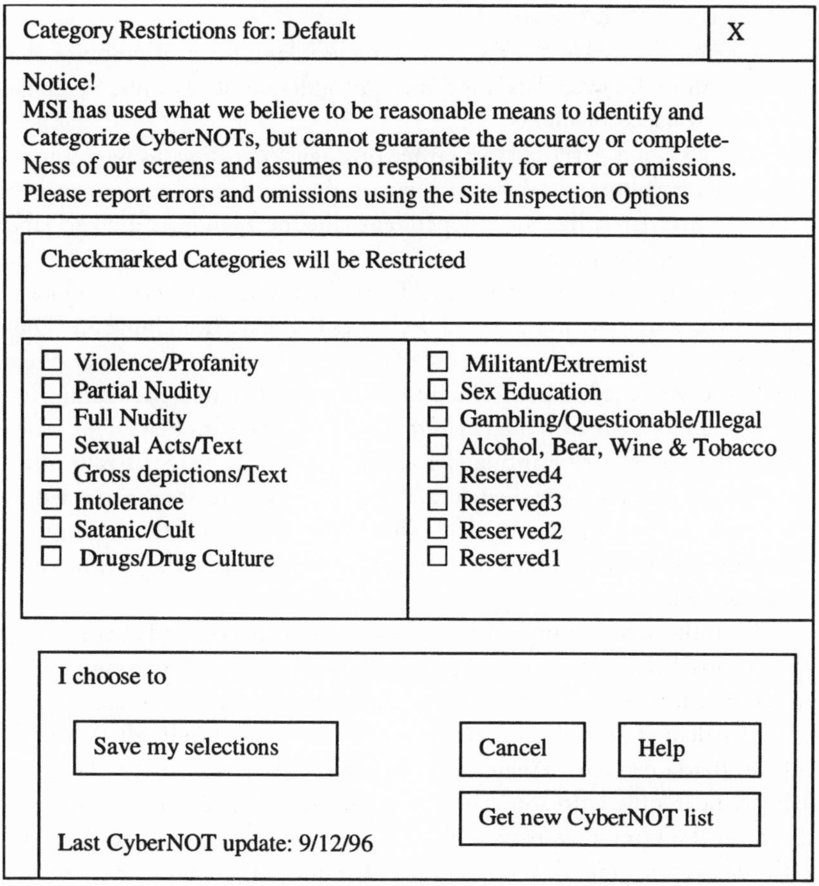

Category Restrictions for: Default	X

Notice!
MSI has used what we believe to be reasonable means to identify and
Categorize CyberNOTs, but cannot guarantee the accuracy or complete-
Ness of our screens and assumes no responsibility for error or omissions.
Please report errors and omissions using the Site Inspection Options

Checkmarked Categories will be Restricted

☐ Violence/Profanity
☐ Partial Nudity
☐ Full Nudity
☐ Sexual Acts/Text
☐ Gross depictions/Text
☐ Intolerance
☐ Satanic/Cult
☐ Drugs/Drug Culture

☐ Militant/Extremist
☐ Sex Education
☐ Gambling/Questionable/Illegal
☐ Alcohol, Bear, Wine & Tobacco
☐ Reserved4
☐ Reserved3
☐ Reserved2
☐ Reserved1

I choose to

| Save my selections | | Cancel | Help |

| Get new CyberNOT list |

Last CyberNOT update: 9/12/96

Figure 4.4 CyberPatrol Category Restriction Menu*

---

extremely aggressive and combative behaviors, or advocacy of unlawful political measures.
10. Sex Education :
    This may include any graphics in any form that advocate the proper
    use of contraceptives.
11. Questionable/Illegal & Gambling :
    Any form of graphic images to promote any activities of a dubious
    nature which may be illegal in any or all jurisdictions.

*CyberPatrol Category Restriction Menu was used by permission of Sun Microsystems Soft-
ware.*

12. Alcohol & Tobacco:

And finally this category may include any form of graphics that promote the sale, consumption, or production of alcoholic beverages and tobacco products.

A Web site is given a label either through *self-rating*, in which individuals place voluntary labels on their products, or *third-party rating*, in which a third party, like an independent labeling agency, is used to label the contents of the products.

Filtering/Blocking Software. Filtering software, also known as blocking software, rates documents and Web sites that have been rated and contain content designated on a filter's "black list." Filters are either client based or server based. Client-based filters are installed on a user computer, and such filters are maintained by individuals. This means that client-based filters offer less security and are prone to tampering. Server-based filters on the other hand are installed centrally on a server and are maintained by a network administrator or an ISP. They are very effective throughout the entire local network and they offer better security because they are not easy to tamper with.

Even though filtering software, both browser based and client based, has recently become very popular, it still has serious problems and drawbacks such as inaccuracies in labeling, restriction on unrated material, and just mere deliberate exclusion of certain Web sites by an individual or individuals. Inaccuracies have many sources. Some Web sites are blocked because they are near a file with some adult content; for example, if some materials are in the same directory as the file with adult content, the Web site with the file without adult content may be blocked. Sometimes Web sites are blocked because they contain words deemed to be distasteful. Such words are sometimes foreign words that have completely different meanings from their English counterparts but that happen to have similar string names. Below are listed the current filtering software packages:

Filter Name	Company	Time Restrictions	Content Restriction	Other Restrictions
CyberPatrol	Microsystems	yes	yes	local PC, TCP/IP
CyberPatrol Corporate	Microsystems	yes	office	local PC, TCP/IP
CyberPatrol Proxy	Microsystems	yes	yes	server level
CYBERsitter	POW! Distribution		alerts & blocks, alerts	local PC, TCP/IP

		monitors/restricts	
Cyber Snoop			restricts e-mail, chat, FTP
daxHOUND	Net Shepard	yes	
I-Guard		yes	server-based language processor
Integro			
Net Nanny	Robinson Marshall, plc	yes	PC, lock, TCP/IP
New View			
SafeSurf			
Solution	SafeSurf	yes	server-based/24 hrs
SurfWatch	Research Machines, plc	yes	PC, email, TCP/IP
Triple Exposure		yes	local PC
WinWatch	Solution Point	yes	user inputs
X-STOP		yes	
Kinder Guard		yes	
Parental Guide		yes	
Bess	N2H2	yes	e-mail, TCP/IP, PC
Websource Internet Solutions	Net Pattern's	yes	e-mail, TCP/IP, PC

As governments and industry executives search for answers to the Internet content problem — governments through political pressures, and industry in an effort to try and limit employee idle time — both are feeling the pressure to filter the Internet. There is a growing sense that in the near future, more and more people will access a filtered or rated Internet.

Public Awareness — Mass Education

The tools to control the Internet have not been limited to hardware and software; they have also included efforts to educate masses of people on the dangers of either regulating the Internet or leaving the Internet unregulated. There have been heated debates on both sides of the issue, between those who advocate some form of control and those who see any form of control as a deathblow to the Internet as we know it today.

Apparently both camps are trying to get as many people on their side as possible. In the process the mass-education train has broken into a number of tracks:

Focused Education. Focused education targets specific groups such as children in schools, professionals, and certain religious and interest groups. Focused education can further be sub-divided into formal education and occasional education.

In formal education the idea is to target the whole length of the education spectrum from kindergarten through college. The focus and contact, however, should be appropriate for the selected level. For example, in elementary education, although it is appropriate to educate kids about the dangers of information misuse and about computer ethics in general, the content and the delivery of that content should be appropriate for that level. In high schools, where there is more maturity and more exploratory minds, the content and of course the delivery system should be more focused and more forceful. This approach changes in colleges because here students are more focused on their majors, and the intended education should reflect this. That is, the content should be directed more towards the professions these young people are planning to enter.

"Occasional education" is that which occurs outside a school setting. Teaching responsible use of information in general and computer ethics in particular is a lifelong process, just as teaching responsible use of a gun should be to a soldier. This responsibility should be and is usually passed on to the professions. Professions enforce this education in a variety of ways. For many traditional professions, this is done through introduction and enforcement of professional codes and guidelines. Other professions supplement their codes by requiring in-service training sessions and refresher courses. Many professions require licensing as a means of ensuring the continuing education of their members.

But having codes and mandating that members live by those codes does not in itself assure that members of those professions will in fact live and abide by those codes. So a kind of enforcement mechanism must be put in place to see that these professionals abide by the codes. There are various ways of enforcing the codes. Some professions use licensure, some use established civil penal code, and some use established mechanisms within the professions to discipline violators. Most professions have clear guidelines for reporting and dealing with grievances, including hearings, censure, and appeals.

Other Education Channels. Other channels of mass education are provided not by focused educational institutions and agencies or by advocacy groups but by individuals, corporations, and agencies using both high technology delivery schemes and traditional mass-circulation media. For example, corporations use postings on covers of their products and on their Web pages to carry educative messages to the general public about issues like security and privacy. Take the case of the U.S. Customs Service International Child Pornography Investigation and Coordination Center. On this agency's Web page is detailed educational material on child pornography. Also many milk processing plants in the United States put missing children on their cartons. These and other private efforts can be productive.

Advocacy

This is a mass-education strategy that has been used since the beginning of humanity. Advocacy groups work with the public, corporations and governments to enhance public education through awareness and peoples' rights. Unlike the focused education campaigns, advocacy education does not distinguish one sector of society from another; rather it is a blanket mass-education campaign. The intended message is passed through mass campaigns, publications in magazines, electronic publications, public events and mass communication media like television, radio and now the Internet.

Advocacy is intended to make people part of the message. For example, during struggles over voting rights in the United States, women's groups and minorities designed and carried out massive advocacy campaigns meant to involve all women, who eventually became part of the movement. Similarly in the minority voting rights struggles, the goal was to involve all minorities whose rights had been denied.

The purpose of advocacy is to organize, build and train so that there is a permanent and vibrant structure that people can be part of. By involving as many people as possible in the campaigns, including the intended audience, the advocacy strategy creates awareness, which leads to more pressure on lawmakers and everyone else responsible. The pressure brought about by mass awareness usually results in some form of action, most times the desired action.

As the Internet has exploded in the last few years, the news media have taken it into the living rooms of almost every family with a television set. With this exposure, people have been able to see the good and the ugly sides of the Internet. The fear created by this exposure made fertile ground for advocacy groups, both pro- and anti–Internet censorship. Having aroused the concern and fear of the public, the advocacy groups went to work. Depending on whether they are pro- or anti–Internet censorship, each advocacy group rallies its troops around an issue of concern. These issues include individual privacy and security, repeal of export control on privacy, better encryption standards, and family values, which include the blocking of pornographic materials and all materials deemed unsuitable for certain audiences. The advocates' lists of issues is growing every day as the Internet gets more exposure.

Besides the advocacy lists of issues getting longer, the number of advocacy groups is also getting larger as more groups are formed in reaction to new issues. Among the most renowned advocacy groups are the following:

Pro–Internet Censorship. *Family Research Council (FRC)*, which works to

- promote and defend traditional family values in all media outlets
- develop and advocate legislative and public policy initiatives that promote and strengthen family and traditional values
- establish and maintain a database for family value research

Enough Is Enough (EE), dedicated to fighting pornography on the Internet

Christian Coalition (CC), which embodies a number of U.S. Christian churches working on legislative issues and strengthening families and family values

The Voter Telecommunication Watch (TVTW), intended to track Internet-related legislation and educate the public about cyberspace.

Anti–Internet Censorship. *American Civil Liberties Union (ACLU)*, the leading U.S. advocacy group of individual rights focused on litigating, legislation and educating the public on issues affecting their individual freedom. Its tasks are based on two principles: that governments are made by the majority through democratic elections and that powers, even those of democratically elected governments, must be limited to ensure individual rights.

Electronic Privacy Information Center (EPIC), a public interest research center in Washington, D.C., U.S., which focuses on emerging civil liberties issues and the protection of privacy, the First Amendment, and other constitutional values. EPIC works mostly through litigation to obtain information for the public concerning privacy policies and to duly inform the public about the activities of governments on these issues.

Privacy International (PI), a U.K.-based advocacy group working as a watchdog on surveillance by governments and corporations. It has spread to over 40 countries to help counter abuse of privacy by raising awareness globally to the dangers of information abuse and misuse in cases such as ID card systems, data marching, military surveillance, and credit card reporting.

Hot lines

The last strategy is to set up hot lines so that ordinary people who are offended or feel that they are threatened by the content of a certain Web site can report it to the selected reporting agency for action. In many countries such agencies are representative groups of ISPs, users and law enforcement agencies. In other countries, like China, these agencies are either law enforcement agencies or government offices.

Conclusions

In the last section we have outlined and sometimes discussed tools in place to check on the activities on the Internet. The array of tools discussed so far indicates the nature of the debate concerning online content and what to do about it. Although there are disagreements on what needs to be done about Internet content, there seems to be total agreement on some issues, such as security and privacy of that content and of those who use cyberspace. On those issues where there is agreement, the tools needed are already in place, although some need improvement. However, on issues where there is no agreement, new and varied tools need to be developed that give customers control of Internet content so that those who feel there is a need for censorship can use those tools, like filters and blockers, to censor this content to the degree they want and those opposed to censorship can live with the content.

Chapter 5

Regulating the Internet: National and Regional Efforts

The global outreach of the Internet has made it a formidable empowering tool for world citizenry. It has lowered barriers to the creation and distribution of content that has been inaccessible to all for generations due to physical national boundaries, thus offering, for the first time in human history, universal access to global resources by all. Although the Internet has afforded these opportunities to the global citizenry and although much Internet content is legitimate business and information, a small but potentially powerful component is harmful and illegal. Although no one can deny that the benefits of the Internet far outweigh this aspect of its content, it has raised disproportional and considerable public, political, economic and legal interests that cannot be ignored. All over the world such interests have caused concern and demands for action and concrete solutions. This call for action has resulted in a scramble by peoples and governments to put barricades around their borders so that they can stop the flow of unwelcome foreign influences. For many communities, and consequently many governments, the Internet is worse than bubonic plague because it threatens the very existence of those governments by exposing the citizenry to foreign ideas and influences. Yet to the zealots of global democracy, the Internet is the most noble thing ever invented. They are, therefore, crusading for an open "border," that is, no censorship of the content of the Internet whatever that content happens to be. They have wrapped themselves in the banners of freedom and free speech. Nationalists and conservatives on the other hand are cracking down hard on the new medium they see as a corrupting, evil carrier of many viruses foreign to their institutions and nations. However, even these nationalists know that they need to harness the new technology for its educational, economic and other advantages. At the same time, however, they realize that the price they have to pay for these advances is high. The realization that these advantages cannot be harnessed unless the technology is allowed to flourish and that the influence of the new technology is devastating to their nations has slowly evolved into a balancing act to find means to encourage the best use of the Internet and at the same time come up with initiatives to prevent its misuse.

In the previous chapter we discussed an array of control tools available to individual citizens, civic groups, governments and regional powers. We saw that these initiatives fall into the following broad regimes:

1. Legislative and policy issues
2. Self-regulation, involving private individuals, like parents and teachers, and private businesses and industries
3. Education, involving mass public awareness through advocacy and professional codes
4. Other tools, involving a collection of sometimes unorthodox techniques and sometimes down-to-earth ones like telephone hot lines

This chapter provides a detailed look at those initiatives as they are being undertaken by multinational and regional organizations like the United Nations and European Union, by national governments, by civic groups and by individuals. Because the initiatives outlined in the previous chapter form an array of measures, there is no uniformity in the way they are applied. In some instances there is more emphasis on legislative measures than on others. And in such cases legislations passed are more restrictive, resulting in cases of censorship. For example, in Singapore and China, as we will see later, the measures taken are very close to censorship. In other instances, like the case of the European Union, measures are more educational, encouraging the general public to be increasingly aware of the issues involved. Such measures are targeted mostly to parents, educators, the public sector and the information industry. The types of measures taken and the degree to which they are applied depend on how seriously the perceived threat is taken. In those countries where the threat perceived is thought to be great, the measures are more restrictive and severe than in countries where the threat is not taken seriously. Each multinational and regional group, national government, civic group and individual has plausible reasons to justify the selected tools. Choices are based on historical, sociopolitical, and security grounds.

Regional and Multinational Efforts

International and regional groupings like the United Nations, European Union, OECD and the G7/P8 many times are composed of governments of selected nations, sometimes with legislative powers but most often with none. The legislations, once passed, usually are binding on member states. However, their implementation depends on the cooperation of individual governments.

Group of Seven/Political Eight (G7/P8)

The Lyon Group, a senior-level group of transnational crime experts representing the G7/P8, is developing legal and technical mechanisms to allow international law enforcement agents to

1. locate, identify and prosecute criminals,
2. create clearing-house procedures in connection with the evidence, and
3. commit resources in training law enforcement agents.

Following the Lyon Group recommendations, on July 30, 1996, the G7/P8 nations — Canada, Britain, France, Japan, Italy, Germany and the United States, with Russia in attendance — met in Paris, France, and agreed on 25 measures to combat international terrorism and related crimes. The group also endorsed a package of Internet control measures including the prohibition and censorship of Internet sources that may contain what they termed "dangerous" information, restriction of Internet speech and imposition of the key escrow encryption. In November of the same year, a group of legal and technical experts in global networks, the Carnegie Group, was formed to catalog Internet acts of misuse and proposed solutions. This standing group is still at work.

The Organization for Economic Cooperation and Development (OECD)

As a result of the efforts by France and Belgium, two members of OECD, the organization is producing a report that urges international cooperation on initiatives and efforts dealing with content and conduct on the Internet. The study undertaken by OECD to produce this report aims to

1. highlight areas of cooperation within member states,
2. define issues that need international cooperation,
3. identify problems, and
4. suggest solutions.

Concerning the distribution of child pornography over the Internet, the OECD Council of Ministers adopted a declaration that strongly condemns those acts and called for measures to fight them. During the ministerial meeting in May 1997 in Paris, France, the ministers endorsed recommendations of the Global Information Infrastructure/Global Information Society report. They further endorsed the OECD cryptography policy guidelines, noting the implications for issues like consumer protection, taxation, commercial transaction, privacy and security on the Internet. The organization is also undertaking a study to compare legislation and policies concerning the Internet.

European Union

The initiatives undertaken by the European Union are broad based and ongoing. They are constantly evolving as new ideas are brought forth and discussions continue. This section looks at a beehive of activities being undertaken by the Union to come up with a definitive set of initiatives agreeable to member states.

At the July 1997 European conference in Bonn, Germany, on the Use of Global Information Networks in Europe, representatives of European leading businesses, user groups, and government ministers of the European Union, the European Commission, European Free Trade Association, countries of Central and Eastern Europe, with representatives from Canada, Japan, Russia and the United States, agreed on promoting initiatives to prevent illegal and harmful Internet content through increasing general awareness among parents, teachers, the public sector and the information industry. These initiatives are in addition to and in conjunction with the *Joint Action to Combat Trafficking in Human Beings and Sexual Exploitation of Children,* adopted by the Council of the European Union in February 1997. See http://www2.echo.lu.best-use/jointact.html for a full text of the document.

The joint action adopted by the council was based on the following two fundamental documents adopted by the European Commission.

(1) *The Green Paper on the Protection of Minors and Human Dignity in Audio Visual and Information Sciences.* The Green Paper examines the challenges to society by audio visual and information sciences with particular focus on the protection of minors and human dignity. It was meant to stimulate public debate over the longer term on the protection of minors and human dignity and to identify problems posed by the misuse of audiovisual and information sciences. It also identifies differences between new and traditional methods of communications. By identifying these differences, the paper attempts to further stimulate debate on appropriate policies suitable for member states. And finally the paper identifies three key themes where policy could be developed:
- Strengthening legal protection
- Encouraging parental control systems
- Improving international cooperation

See http://www2.echo.lu/legal/en/internet/content/gpen.txt.html#intro for a full text of this document.

(2) *Communication on Illegal and Harmful Content on the Internet,* gives policy options for action to fight against harmful and illegal content on the Internet. See http://www2.echo.lu/legal/en/internet/communic.html for a full text of this document.

The resolutions by the commission on both the *Green Paper* and the *Communication on Illegal and Harmful Content on the Internet* follow the resolution adopted by the Telecommunication Council of Ministers in November 1996, itself based on an earlier report of the Commission Working Party on illegal and harmful content on the Internet. The Telecommunication Council adopted the following recommendations (1):

1. Member states should
   - Encourage and facilitate self-regulatory systems, including representative bodies for Internet service providers and users, effective codes of conduct and possibly hot-line reporting mechanisms available to the public
   - Encourage the provision to users of filtering mechanisms and the setting up of rating systems; for instance the PICS (Platform for Internet Content Selection) standard launched by the international World-Wide-Web consortium with EC support should be promoted

- Participate actively in the International Ministerial Conference hosted by Germany and encourage attendance by representatives of the actors concerned

2. The Commission, as far as Community competencies are concerned, should
    - Ensure the coherence of work and follow-up of the measures suggested in the above-mentioned report, taking into account other relevant work in this field and reconvene the Working Party as necessary to monitor progress and take further initiatives if appropriate
    - Foster coordination at community level of self-regulatory and representative bodies
    - Promote and facilitate the exchange of information on best practice in this area
    - Foster research into technical issues, in particular filtering, rating, tracing and privacy enhancing, taking into account Europe's cultural and linguistic diversity
    - Consider further the question of legal liability for Internet content

3. The commission, in the framework of community competencies, and member states take all necessary steps to enhance the effectiveness of the measures referred to in this resolution through international cooperation, building on the results of the International Ministerial Conference and in discussions in other international fora.

The Commission is drawing up an Action Plan on Illegal and Harmful Content on the Internet based on the work of the Telecommunication Council and the Working Party. This plan will then be sent to the Telecommunication Council for review. The whole exercise is ongoing, but the common theme of all the commission's work is to promote initiatives aimed at increasing general awareness among parents, educators, public users and the information industry about how to deal with Internet issues. Such initiatives are grouped under the following categories:

1. Encouraging and facilitating self-regulatory systems, including information industry bodies like ISPs, developing effective codes of conduct by professional and civic organizations and setting up public hot lines and other reporting mechanisms
2. Encouraging the use of filtering mechanisms and the setting up of rating systems like the Platform for Internet Content Selections (PICS)
3. Fostering closer cooperation between member states on the international level
4. Fostering research in technical issues (like rating, filtering, tracking

and privacy enhancement) that reflects Europe's cultural and linguistic diversity

Taking these initiatives as a basis, the European Union's commissioner for telecommunications, Martin Bangermann, has called for a global Internet charter. The charter, according to the commissioner, would deal with questions of technical standards, illegal content, licenses, encryption and data privacy on a global basis. The charter, as it is envisioned, would preempt a likely mosaic of different rules adopted by individual countries and many international organizations. And except for a few exceptions like child pornography and terrorism, the charter would not impose global rules but would recognize existing international organizations' jurisdictions and would draw from their efforts

Individual Countries

In September 1995 the Information Highway Advisory Council of Canada issued a report entitled "Connection, Community, Content: The Challenge of the Information Highway" (2). The report examined proposals on controlling offensive and illegal content on the Internet. The work of the council and the report it produced is but one of the many deliberations and reports by such bodies from many countries as they try to come up with some kind of framework acceptable to a broad segment of their respective audiences. These deliberations also indicate a wide range of opinion on the question of regulating the Internet. A number of initiatives have been taken by different countries, and many more are under consideration, but they all can be grouped into the following categories:

1. Legislative, involving illegal and policy issues. Governments are introducing new legislations and or amending existing ones to suit the perceived crimes
2. Self-regulatory systems, encouraging industry, civic groups, and professional organizations to come up with regulatory frameworks like codes, bylaws, and canons
3. Rating systems, involving individual parents, teachers, company executives and everybody else. Once rating systems are developed then filtering and blocking software can be used
4. Development of hardware schemes, involving encryption standards and networks schemes

5. Licensing and or requiring service providers to comply with stated conditions

6. Advocacy groups and hot lines, involving the formation of advocacy groups and the setting up of hot lines

Countries have used these initiatives to suit their respective citizens' needs and demands. What follows is a discussion of what has been done to date in individual countries.

Britain

I will start this discussion with the remarks of a British colleague, Diane Whitehouse, who wrote to me to summarize what has been done in the U.K. She says that the initiatives so far undertaken in the U.K. are not legislative but are more self-regulatory in terms of constraining the role of Internet service providers. She believes that "the government was/is loathe to take action legislatively."

Legislation

Diane Whitehouse's remarks are supported by the views of Granges, a British professional lawyer, who believes that current U.K. legislation adequately covers Internet use, and also the view of Barbara Roche, a British government DTI minister responsible for Internet use, who said that the U.K. government is working in close cooperation with the Home Office, the Metropolitan Police and the Internet Service Providers (ISP) to facilitate the development of a system dealing with illegal content on the Internet, using existing laws and penalties (3, 30). Among such current legislation Granges referred to are the following:

1. Obscene Publication Act (1959) — amended
2. Criminal Justice and Public Order Act (1994) — amended
3. The Protection of Children Act (1978) — amended
4. The Criminal Justice Act 1988 — amended: Section 188 of this Act, for example, makes it an offense for an individual to be in possession of any indecent photograph or pseudophotograph of a child. The term *pseudophotograph* covers all images, computer generated or otherwise, including stored data that can have an appearance or can be converted into a photograph.
5. Defamation Act (1996): Section 1 of this Act codifies and expands the defense of innocent dissemination to cover ISPs, printers and broad-

casters in case of unrecorded statements by persons for whose actions the broadcaster is not responsible.

6. Sexual Offenses (Conspiracy and Incitement) Act (1996): This also broadly covers incitement in the context of transnational child abuse. For example, it makes it illegal to incite another person to commit certain sexual acts against children abroad by any means, including telephone, fax, Internet and other similar methods.

Self-Regulation

According to Diane Whitehouse, U.K. Internet providers were among the first in Europe to set up professional self-regulating bodies. The formation of these bodies was started by what many believe was a letter from the Club and Vice Unit of the London Metropolitan Police Force to ISPs in the U.K., supplying them with a list of groups that the chief of police believed contained pornographic materials and asking the ISPs to monitor the newsgroups and decide by themselves what actions to take.

Following this letter, the U.K. government bodies, including the DTI, London Metropolitan Police and the Home Office, together with civic and industry representative organs including Safety-Net Foundation and the two major U.K. Internet Providers Associations — the U.K. Internet Service Providers Association (ISPA) and the London Internet Exchange (LINX) — agreed on a set of proposals commonly known as "R³-Safety-Net: Rating, Reporting and Responsibility for Child Pornography and Illegal Material on the Internet." R³-Safety-Net proposals were based on five principles (4):

1. The Internet is not a legal vacuum. In general the law applies to all activities on the Internet in the same way it applies to all other issues. If something is illegal online, it is probably illegal off-line as well.

2. The issues being dealt with are neither free speech nor censorship but are concerned with materials and activities that society views as unacceptable.

3. ISPs must bear their part of the responsibility by implementing reasonable, practicable and proportionate measures to hinder the use of the Internet for illegal purposes and provide an environment where it is possible to identify illegal materials and activities. To this end R³-Safety-Net proposals recommend that Internet service providers offer strong protection and responsible policies in those areas where there is an urgency, like in World Wide Web (WWW) and Usenet newsgroups. WWW policies should include the following:

- promoting PICS-enabled software for accessing the WWW
- requiring all their users to rate their own Web pages using RSACi
- removing Web pages hosted on their servers that are persistently and deliberately misrated
- removing Web pages hosted on their servers that are identified and verified to them as containing child pornography (or other illegal material) if the users fail to cooperate by removing them themselves

And the policies in Usenet newsgroups should also include the following:

- supporting the development of a new Internet standard for transmitting ratings for newsgroups according to their "normal content"
- supporting the availability of rating sources for all Usenet groups
- modifying news servers to deliver group ratings to end-user software when the standard becomes available
- promoting PICS-enabled news software when available
- removing from their servers, within a reasonable time period, news articles identified and verified to them as containing illegal material

R^3-Safety-Net proposals also prompt the users to take their share of the responsibility for their activities on the Internet. Such user responsibility could be enforced through providing traceability of those irresponsible users to close the abuse of the anonymity facility on the Internet. To these, the ISPs should work with any designated organization to close any known loopholes and to identify and investigate all appropriate measures to provide facilities for better traceability. ISPs should also ensure that anonymous servers they operate in the U.K. record details of identity so that such details can be made available to the police.

4. ISPs should be able to offer protection to end users and themselves by hindering the availability of child pornography and see it removed from the Internet

5. There is an established law in any country to determine what materials or activities are illegal.

The proposals also called for an independent foundation to oversee and support the adoption of the three Rs: Responsibility based on Rating and Reporting of illegal materials.

To implement the R^3-Safety-Net proposals, an independent organization called the Internet Watch Foundation (IWF) was formed in 1996 to address the problems of illegal Internet content. The agenda of IWF was to enhance the potential of the Internet to inform, educate, entertain and conduct business by

- hindering transmission on the Internet of illegal content materials
- encouraging the classification of legal materials transmitted through the Internet, thus enabling users to customize the Internet content to their needs (5)

Besides the major players, other industry and civic self-regulatory bodies are forming, including the Cyber Angels from Los Angeles, a U.S. export of the vigilante group, the Guardian Angels.

Use of Rating Systems

The IWF is currently working with industries in the U.K., representatives from children's charities, ISPs, the media and civil liberties groups to develop a rating system relevant to U.K. Internet users. Besides locally developing rating systems, users in the U.K. can get access to widely used rating systems developed internationally. The IWF is also creating inroads to foster international cooperation, building contacts and making relationships with organizations with similar interests so that action, mostly jointly, can be taken in countries where objectionable materials originate.

Hardware/Technical Solutions

IWF is working with ISPs to develop rating systems and other hardware initiatives applicable at the server level, like firewalls, to deal with information security and content issues.

Advocacy/Hot lines

IWF has set up telephone hot lines and encouraged users to report materials they deem to be illegal. Besides telephone hot lines, IWF has also established fax and e-mail hot lines. Other advocacy groups are forming, including the Digital Diversity — a loose organization of individuals promoting the use of the Internet by lesbians, gays and bisexuals — and overseas organizations like those in the United States and Canada.

France

France, like the U.K., has put more emphasis on a self-regulatory Internet, echoing the policy of the European Union, although a number of legal initiatives are still in place and more are in the works.

Legislation

France's legislative efforts parallel to some extent those of the United States. Like the United States with its Communication Decency Act fiasco, France had its version of this fiasco in the Telco Act. On July 24, 1996, France's Conseil Constitutionnel, France's High Court, struck down the Telco Act, stating that articles 43-2 and 43-3 within Article 15 of the Act were unconstitutional. Article 15, best known as "Amendment No. 200," or the Fillon's Amendment, after François Fillon, Minister of Posts, Telecommunications and Space, was drawn up to control the Internet. This amendment comprised three articles: 43-1, 43-2 and 43-3. According to the Association des Utilisateurs d'Internet (AUI) (Organization of Internet Users), who filed the winning lawsuit, Article 15 of this amendment was "hasty, useless, unjustifiable, technically inapplicable and dangerous to democracy and freedom of expression" (6).

More specifically:

1. Article 43-1 obliges ISPs to offer means to their clients to restrict Internet access.
2. Article 43-2 selected government agencies to oversee the activities of Internet, placing Conseil Superieur de la Telematique (CST) under the authority of Conseil Superieur de l'Audiovisuel (CSA) and granted CST with advisory privileges.
3. Article 43-3 required ISPs to assume the responsibilities of publishers and ensure a priori control of the information they receive, store and redistribute over the Internet. For a full text of the Fillon's Amendment see http://www.aui.fr/Dossiers/Amend-fillon/Presentation.html (in French).

Besides legislation failures, France also tried enforcement of Internet discipline using existing laws. French laws forbid the use of the Internet, just like all other media, for racist and anti–Semitic propaganda and sexual exploitation of children. Also since the 1990 legislation, France banned encrypted communication with the exception of the military. Using these laws, in May 1996 the Section de Rercherche (the research unit) of the Gendarmerie charged two ISP managers of FranceNet and WorldNet for receiving, storing and redistributing "pictures with a pedophilic content" (7). The materials in question were distributed on alt.binaries newsgroups.

The government has also been pushing hard for international cooperative initiatives, resulting in the following initiatives:

1. The 1996 Telecommunication Ministry proposal for an international

convention to deal with problems faced by legislators in dealing with the global nature of the Internet.

2. The 1996 draft entitled "Agreement on International Cooperation with Regard to the Internet" to the OECD ministerial conference to establish a code of conduct and to require OECD member states to ensure that Internet users in their jurisdictions comply with all national laws in regards to
   • respect of human dignity,
   • protection of privacy,
   • consumer protection, and
   • protection of copyrights.

3. Participation by government and government agencies in efforts by international bodies like WTO, EU, WIPO, OECD, UNESCO, and G7/P8.

Self-Regulation

After the defeat of the Fillon's Amendment, France changed course in its effort to regulate the Internet, stressing more self-regulation. French prime minister Lionel Jospin, in his speech "Preparing France's Entry into the Information Society," stressed this, pointing out that "Internet actors should assume responsibility for preventative regulations of the network" and that such regulation should be "based on rules of conduct and Deontology" and must be balanced and offer full respect for freedom of communication (8).

The French self-regulatory approach parallels that of the U.K., revolving around an established institution with (a) a strong monitoring role with regards to legal, political, social and economic aspects of the Internet and (b) some authority in mediation following established national laws and agreed-on guidelines.

However, unlike in the U.K., where such an institution, the IWF, is already in place, France's Association des Utilisateurs d'Internet (Organization of Internet Users) has a limited mandate to promote the development and democratization of the use of electronic networks, and its role is more as advocate than as an Internet watchdog. Further, unlike the U.K.'s approach, the French self-regulatory initiatives are likely to revolve around the new draft Internet charter or Charte de l'Internet* after it is discussed and passed. The Internet Charter aims to facilitate (9)

Permission to use the French version of this Charte was granted by Nicolas Ros de Lochounoff, Direction Juridique, TRANSICIEL.

- the harmonious development of the Internet
- the establishment of laws and treaties to apply to all Internet players
- self-regulation, by using simple tools

The Charter covers any Internet user satisfying the following criteria:

- live within Internet domain name ".fr"
- live on French territory around the world
- have conventional link with at least one organization resident on French territory in the course of their Internet business
- provide information for Internet access specifically for French residents

Here is the full text of the Charter in English translation.*

Proposition for an Internet Charter

Rules and Courtesies of the Actors of the Internet in France

1997

Presentation: for the Self-Regulation of the Internet

The rapid development of networks worldwide such as the Internet constitutes an extraordinary collective treasure but revealed excesses which have raised concern in public opinion.

Two categories of "actors" are particularly exposed: the users, through lack of knowledge or misconceptions of the legal responsibilities associated with the furnishing of contents, and the Internet Service Providers (ISPs) by virtue of a presumed responsibility by providing access to information.

The Internet is foremost a network of users. However, far from mere consumers, they are veritable "actors" of the Internet.

In the course of creation and cultural activities, through participation in group projects (partnerships), volunteering, and individual initiatives, they are the life-blood of the social activities of the Internet.

This essential role of users gives them certain rights but also certain responsibilities.

Numerous problems encountered on the Internet have a novel make-up which makes national laws hard to apply to them. Rather than facing a legal vacuum, Internet "actors" are confronted with a multiplicity of existing rules and regulations which must be applied concurrently. These rules, often originally intended for businesses or partnerships, henceforth apply to individuals who do not necessarily have sufficient legal training.

*The English translation of this Charter was done by Dr. Victoria Steinberg, Foreign Languages Department, University of Tennessee, Chattanooga. E-mail: Victoria-Steinberg@utc.edu

It is advisable to contribute to offering everyone a more receptive entry into the new complexities of the information society and an unimpeded working-out of the practices organizing relationships within the information society.

To do so, the "Actors of the Internet" deem it necessary to clarify, affirm and make public with this Internet Charter the rules and practices to be respected as much between themselves as between themselves and French society in general.

The Actors of the Internet are instituting an Internet Council, an independent and unique body for self-regulation and mediation.

The action of this body aims to insure:
— the evolution of the present Charter through recommendations;
— an informative and advisory role with the Actors;
— arbitration between Actors;
— issuance of notices to Actors after charges have been brought by one of the members, a third party or through self-regulation;
— co-operation with French authorities or their foreign counterparts in cases where they are the deemed representative.

Towards the goal of assuring equal treatment of all Actors, the body is carrying out the centralization and the concerted appraisal of complaints.

The Charter, Notices and Recommendations outlined by the Internet Council can have legal value.

The Actors of the Internet state firmly their commitment to uphold this new space of expression and liberty opened to us by the Internet. They also assert that the exercising of that liberty must be practiced in strict respect for the human being, especially those in their youth.

I. DEFINITIONS

The definitions below are subject to development or revision under the control of the Internet Council, notably according to the state of technology and the actual practices on the networks.

For the application of the present Charter, the following definitions were agreed upon:

Internet: Collection of interactive networks, open or interconnected, relaying computers.

A. Functions of the Internet

User: anyone accessing the Internet with the goal of consultation or private correspondence. The user thus understood is not subject to the obligations of the present Charter.

Internet Actor: any physical or moral person, professional or not, using the Internet for purposes other than mere consultation and utilizing one of the functions of the Internet defined below.

An Internet Actor can exercise several functions, concomitantly or successively. Under the present Charter, the Actor will assume, alternatively or cumulatively according to each case, the agreements and responsibilities proper to each of his or her functions. It is thus agreed to distinguish between Internet Actors according to their respective activities on the networks at any given instant (notably reading, posting, modifying, lodging, and transmitting of content) to which correspond, for technical or legal reasons, distinct actions, duties, and responsibilities.

Providers of infrastructure ("Telcos"): Those who provide the "conduit" necessary to access the Internet or to use the Internet.

Providers of access (ISPs): Those who provide access to the Internet by the Intermediary of their computers ("gateways") which themselves are tied into the Internet, including the putting into place of replications of sites ("mirroring") and the putting into place of applicable relays ("proxy servers").

Providers of lodging (Content Custodians): Those who compile and process content on computers connected to the Internet and who make it available to the public.

Providers of infrastructure, access, and lodging are collectively designated as "technical providers."

Providers of content: Those who furnish content for sites, or data sets or chat rooms in order to make that content available to the public on the Internet. Providers of merchandise (the press, editors, bankers, salespersons) are distinguished from providers of non-sales type content (university affiliates, researchers, individuals...).

B. Internet Services

Listservs: spaces for thematic discussion prerecorded and relayed through the network to those sites subscribing to those forums.

Chat rooms: discussion spaces (often thematic) functioning in real time, exchanging messages through the network to all of the sites subscribing to these services.

Electronic mail: electronic communication of private messages, with or without attachment(s)(text or file) which permits the sending to one or more person(s) identified by individual information, data or their works.

Remote sites: computerized sites which make available content accessible by remote login or file transfer protocol (FTP).

C. Other Definitions

Broadcasting: making content available to users and/or providers as yet unidentified.

Content: any information, data, work, or service made available to the public.

Cases of flagrant copying of protected material and flagrant breaching of Internet courtesies are equally prohibited.

Sensitive content: Content which, without being manifestly illicit, is by nature offensive to the sensibilities of certain people.

Contestable action: action which by nature has an undesirable effect on the functioning of the Internet.

Hypertext link: mechanism of local reference in, or produced by, a source or content which permits direct access to another content (target) wherever it may be. This mechanism allows instantaneous passage via highlighted text in a Web page to another Web page, wherever its location in the network.

Electronic address: combination of characters allowing identification of an addressee of electronic mail.

II. GOAL OF THE CHARTER

In order to encourage harmonious development of the Internet, the goal of the Charter is to specify, within the framework of laws and treaties, the rules and courtesies for Actors of the Internet and to facilitate its use by a simple and practicable tool of self-regulation, the Council of the Internet.

Those Actors covered by the Charter of the Internet must meet one of the following criteria:

— any Actor whose domain is "fr" without prejudice to other types of designations as to domain;
— any Actor of the Internet in the French territory and providing the means or services, or the creation or provision to the public of content on the Internet;
— any Internet Actor assuming one of these functions and having established an active conventional relationship with at least one Actor residing in the French territory;
— any Internet Actor in the course of whose activity or content furnished are specifically aimed at French residents or those providing access to a French resident.

III. GENERAL PRINCIPLES

A. Adherence to the Charter

By adhering to the Charter, the Actors promise to respect its arrangements;

And, as for professional Actors, they promise, in addition:

— to promote or further usage of the Charter and to develop conditions for its use;
— to use contracts which make reference to the Internet Charter;
— to create on their respective home pages a link to the Council of the Internet;

— to revise, on a daily basis, their e-mail so that it reinforces the goals of the Charter.

B. Obligation to Clarity

Any Actor making content available to the public will furnish an electronic address allowing contact with him or her or his or her representative so that any problem can be communicated regarding the available content.

In the case of professionals or moral people, they will in addition furnish legal identification (name or social denomination, nature of the organization, capital or SIREN number, or site address). And, in the case of the press, the above references are complemented by specific information (the name of the director of the publication and of those responsible for editing, of the legal representative of the company and of its three principal associates, as well as, if applicable, the number[s] of joint commission of publications to which the service is linked).

IV. INTERNET COUNCIL

The Actors of the Internet are creating a self-regulating body, the Internet Council (hereafter the Council), which conforms to the spirit of the Charter such that, in the continuation of its tradition and its history, the Internet continue to be regulated by its own Actors.

Any Actor is considered a member in the eyes of the Council.

A. Missions

The missions of the Council are, within the framework of the Charter, information, prevention, and regulation.

The action of the Council aims specifically to assure:

— the evolution of the present Charter through recommendations;
— an informational and advisory role through Actors and Users;
— mediation between Actors;
— the provision of notices to Actors in light of any decisions brought to bear in applying the Charter whether action was brought by a member, a third party or automatically;

To guarantee uniformity and equality of treatment to all Actors, the Charter seeks centralization and a unified effort to fully appreciate and understand all claims.

The Council uses any form of cooperation necessary, notably other national authorities concerned.

The Council works to develop international cooperation with organizations located in other nations having similar objectives, such that the international character of the Internet will not be a hindrance to the successful functioning of regulation.

B. Composition

The Actors of the Internet supporting the Charter are designated according to their activity or their quality as representative to the administrative council:

The Council is composed of the following representatives of Actors of the Internet:

— Internet Service Providers of a non-profit nature (University affiliates, Researchers, User Associations, Representatives of Public Information Providers);
— Internet Service Providers for profit (the Press, Editors, Banks, Merchants);
— Providers of Infrastructure (Telcos)
— Providers of Access (ISPs)
— Providers of Lodging (Content Custodians)

The presidency will be filled by someone independently elected by the Council.

Representatives from the general public and information professionals will constitute the administrative council.

V. NOTICE RELATING TO THE CONTENT AND TO MANIFESTLY ILLICIT ACTIONS

1. The Internet Council receives claims from Users, Actors, and third parties relating to the content or actions whose manifest content is allegedly illicit. Actions can be automatic.

Claims submitted anonymously to the Internet Council will be kept secret.

2. If the Council finds the content or action illicit, in terms of the present Charter, the Internet Council will advise the author or responsible party to modify or eliminate said content or action.

3. If the author or responsible party of content or action found to be illicit has not removed this content or modified this action within a reasonable period, the Internet Council will tender an advisory statement recommending that technicians remove or block access to this content.

4. Technicians receiving such an advisory agree to furnish the Internet Council with information and explanations responding to the advisory. All advisories are confidential, unless forbidden by law.

5. Technicians inform their clients of their power to suspend service in providing manifestly illicit content to the public according to the Notice of the Internet Council.

6. The Internet Council will inform its members of juridical decisions which have as their object interdiction of content.

VI. SENSITIVE CONTENT

The Actors undertake to promote the mechanisms which permit users to select material based upon their own (level of) sensitivity.

Thus, the Actors under the present Charter promise to:

A. Promote, within reasonable measure, the availability and utilization by parents and other responsible parties of a supervisory nature the logistical means to filter content based upon the "Platform of Internet Content Selection" (PICS Standards).

In particular, those who furnish pornographic and/or violent content agree to identify their content as such, according to the PICS Standards.

B. To promote, within reasonable measure, the classification of Internet sites by third parties into categories based on content.

C. To promote the implementation of a process to obtain similar results advocated by the Internet Council.

If necessary, the Internet Council is free to recommend regarding the adaptation of any existing system.

A. Principles

1. The respect of human dignity entails the protection of human life and the rejection of any form of discrimination on the basis of views, origin, and/or ethnic, social, religious, political, union, sexual or health-related membership or not, true or presumed.

2. Protection of minors entails the rejection of any form of exploitation of minors, especially sexual.

B. Specific Tenet

On the basis of applicable laws, the Actors promise not to create on French territory content contrary to human dignity or public order.

VIII. FREEDOMS AND FUNDAMENTAL RIGHTS

A. Principles

The fundamental rights and freedoms include in particular:
— free speech,
— the right to information,
— individual freedom,
— freedom of association, even virtual,
— protection of privacy, including automated access of data and rights to graphic representations,
— security,
— the privacy of correspondence,
— property rights, including intellectual.

B. Specific Tenets

1. General steps

Providers of access will inform clients of principal risks inherent in the use of the Internet relating to the violation of privacy of correspondence, copyrighted and personal data.

The Internet Council will make available to the public notifications relating to means and products intended to guarantee the confidentiality and integrity of their correspondence and information (in particular regarding means of encryption after receiving required authorization).

2. Privacy of correspondence

Private correspondence on the Internet is confidential.

Employers of personnel with access to computers connected to or as elements of a network which handle correspondence promise to safeguard the confidentiality of their employees regarding private correspondence which they might know of through work, and they promise to make employees aware of penalty in cases of violation of that privacy.

3. Protection of privacy

On the Internet, Users have a right to privacy and anonymity.

This anonymity can be assured through the use of anonymous remailers for e-mail and display of content as well as for access to content.

These services must assure and preserve the means to contact people who have access to the data base of anonymous electronic addresses.

The codes, dates, and hours of access to the Internet can, however, be protected by the Providers of access in order to protect network users from intrusions.

The use of automated personal information (like the use of "cookies")by Actors of the Internet will undergo strict application of the agreed-upon responsibilities, such as principles of loyalty and clarity, respect for outcomes, security, and rights of access.

Towards that goal, every Actor will allow Users, with strict legal limits, to know the nature of data collected by the Actor via the computer about them.

IX. PROTECTION OF THE RIGHTS OF INTELLECTUAL PROPERTY

A. Principles

Distinctive signs, inventions or original creations are subject to protection as intellectual property. Subject to legal exception, exploitation/utilization on the Internet of such creations presupposes procurement, according to the entitlements of moral and patrimonial rights, of the rights and/or authorizations required by law.

Copyrights are applicable to Actors of the Internet.

Authors of data bases are also protected under the European Union, either by copyright or another specific right.

Finally, specific mention of authors of works, as holder of rights, and of numerical identification of works cannot be overlooked or modified without the consent of the Author and/or those representing his/her rights.

B. Specific Tenets

The Providers of content must ascertain all rights and/or necessary authorizations. Providers of lodging (Content Custodians) must include in their contract(s) with their client(s) a clause which draws attention to this principle.

Before using any sign on the Internet to distinguish a product or service or to designate the address of a site, the person using that sign must diligently undertake to guarantee the availability of that sign or to disclose its source.

Providers of lodging (Content Custodians) promise to make contractual arrangements with their client(s) regarding the fate of custodial data once the contract is terminated or expired.

X. PROTECTION OF CONSUMERS

A. Principles

The Actors of the Internet do not intend either to substitute this Charter for the rules, courtesies and other ethical texts which govern the commercial activities which may develop on the Internet, nor do they intend to undermine free trade or freedom of trade.

B. Specific Tenets

1. Electronic commerce

Actors conducting electronic commerce (ecommerce) on the Internet with French consumers, excluding Technical Providers, agree to furnish the following information in an accessible manner:

— the essential characteristics of the product or service offered. They agree in particular to guarantee that the description of said product or service is not of a misleading character or nature;
— the actual price, as well as charges and accessory costs, specifically delivery charges or taxes;
— the terms of the sale or supply of applicable service;
— the complete legal identity of the seller or the Provider of the service; in particular, mention of name brand and/or product and/or company name, SIREN number, if applicable, company (headquarters) address

and the business responsible for the transaction, relevant telephone numbers and/or e-mail addresses of those in charge of the transaction;

The acceptance of a transaction presumes an immediate binding contract between parties;

The Actors of the Internet will make a concerted effort to define those means which best allow consumers who have expressly chosen to protect themselves against automated unsolicited selling via e-mail.

Technical Providers agree to conduct their business honestly and loyally with French consumers.

2. Technical Providers

If a specific system, exclusive of the one described above in section 1, is put in place concerning the commercial actions of Technical Providers, the system must clearly provide the following information:

— legal identification;
— rates (for installation, subscription, and hourly rates for various services);
— types of services offered according to their essential characteristics;
— information which allows the consumer to know the necessary configuration in order to benefit from the services offered by the provider;
— length of contract(s) and the legal and technical conditions of termination of contract(s), if it is not for immediate service, as well as the consequences;
— the conditions for transfer of contract to different addresses or e-mail or home pages in the case of a change of providers.

Providers of lodging (Content Custodians) will, in addition, furnish the following:

— the amount and storage capacity available to the client for files and specifically the circumstances under which data can be found erased by the Provider of access or lodging;

Providers of access must also furnish the following information:

— if necessary, conditions for help;
— the means to legally download screening or filtering software.

XI. IN-HOUSE MEDIATION PROCEDURES

The Actors of the Internet will try to mediate amiably.

Before bringing charges on another Actor, The Actors of the Internet will seek settlement by asking for reconciliation, mediation or arbitrage by the Council, except where contact with the Actor is impossible, or in cases where immediate legal action is required.

Actors involved in litigation or investigation regarding facts relevant to the Charter can communicate pertinent Notices relating to said litigation or said investigation to all parties involved.

This charter was a result of the working group established by the Post and Telecommunication Ministry. Its focus is on educating users and ISPs to avoid legal proceedings through

1. establishing the code of conduct in the use of the Internet
2. defining the principal players in cyberspace, like Internet Service Providers (ISPs) and other types of users
3. defining the areas of application of the charter within the framework of the Internet
4. declaring the importance of
   - human dignity
   - protection of minors
   - rights and freedoms
   - protection of intellectual property rights
   - consumer protection

Hot Line/Advocacy

The advocacy role is currently mostly done by the AUI, the French Internet Service Providers Association.

Germany

Unlike the other European countries and the European Union, Germany has been more aggressive towards fighting what they deem to be bad Internet content. Most German efforts have been in areas of legislation and enforcement of new and existing legislations, focusing on explicit materials and hate speeches, most notably anti–Semitic and neo–Nazi materials.

Legislation

The mode that drives the legislative part of the Internet agenda in Germany can be summarized from the words of Rita Suessmuth, president of the Bundestag, the German Parliament. According to Suessmuth, "Freedom of expression reaches its limits when human dignity is violated and violence is promoted" (10). Although her comments were directed at all forms of communication media, her immediate concern was the Internet when she said that the Internet "must not be allowed to become a forum for those who defile children" (10). This explains a series of activities authorities in Germany have been engaged in, both legislative and enforcement. On the enforcement front, efforts are led by the German Public Prosecutor's Office based on existing German laws. The list of high-profile prosecutions so far include the 1994–95 CompuServe case, in which around 200 Usenet newsgroups were blocked for having bad material; the 1996 Deutsche Telekom (DT), blocking T-Online network from certain Web sites for anti–Semitic materials; the 1996 federal government pressure on Deutche Forschungsnets, a major academic ISP, to block a Dutch Web site, www.xs4all.nl, when it listed a Web page of the magazine *Radikal*, which was burned in Germany; the filing of charges by the federal government against a member of the Communist Party of Democratic Socialism for linking to the *Radikal* magazine; and the blocking of www.serve.com. Besides blocking sites, the Public Prosecutor's Office has carried out a number of investigations into the activities and contents of Internet service providers and individual users like the Hamburg investigation of America Online.

Legislation-wise, a number of bills have been passed dealing with information and communication service providers. These legislations are split between the German federal government and the Lander. The federal government legislations cover interactive services that involve a combination of data to form text, images and sound that are transmitted. These legislations include the Information and Communication Services Act (1997). The Act, according to Michael Schelider, stipulates the following (11):

- The responsibility of the service providers is stipulated in accordance with general laws.
- Service providers who merely provide data for usage without storing it in their own domains are not responsible for the contents of this data. An automatic intermediate storage that is not permanent and that automatically deletes the data after a certain time period is not deemed to be storage in the meaning of item 1 above.
- Service providers are not responsible for outside content that they keep ready for usage without having an influence on it unless the content is known to them and they have the technical capabilities to prevent its dissemination.
- Service providers are obligated to bar unlawful contents in a teleservice upon the request of the public prosecutor if this is technologically feasible and reasonable.

Also in April 1996 the German Parliament started debating the "Federal Law to Regulate the Conditions for Information and Communications

Services (IUDG)" bill. According to Armin Medosch, paragraphs 85 and 87 of this bill require all online and telecom service providers (ISPs) to provide backdoors to the state to get access to the data of their users. In carrying out this law, ISPs bear the costs for providing the technical structure for the state (12).

The Lander has jurisdiction over and passes legislations to cover services intended for the general public and all on-demand services as long as they are communicated en masse. Among such legislations is the state treaty on media services signed by the heads of government of Landers in early 1997. Lander legislations are based on two premises: (a) that states set the standards and carry out controls, and (b) that ISPs and individual users bear some responsibility. Their cooperation with the state is essential, and all legislations set out precisely the responsibilities of ISPs for the content transmitted.

Self-Regulation

Like British and French ISPs, German ISPs play a leading role in the self-regulation initiatives of the Internet. However, unlike their colleagues in the U.K. and France, German ISPs are more involved in the government efforts. The main German self-regulatory body is the Internet Content Task Force (ICTF). ICTF was formed out of the Electronic Commerce Forum (ECO), a German ISPs body and the Media Council consisting of ISPs, politicians, lawyers, Internet users and media representatives. ICTF's action plan involves

- documenting the traffic in news on a central server from information provided by the ISPs. The selected information is stored on CD-ROMs and regularly given to an attorney or notary public for safe keeping;
- generating political pressure to bring awareness of global problems that can be tackled by international cooperation;
- constantly looking over the contents of Usenet, without examining them in detail and making recommendations to be sent to the ISPs. Recommendations may include things like certain newsgroups not distribute specific articles. Failure to do this by an ISP who carries the newsgroup may result in citation. For example, an ISP can be found guilty of aiding and abetting criminal activities if it failed to act after it had been informed about the URL with illicit document by ICTF.

The Netherlands — Holland

The most loose and lightly industry-based initiatives in Europe are found in Holland. The government has long encouraged self-regulatory and industry-based initiatives, so the Dutch collaborative efforts are among the Dutch Foundation for Internet Providers (NLIP), the Dutch Internet Users, the National Bureau Against Racial Discrimination (NBRD), the National Criminal Intelligence Service (CRI) and the Dutch Police (DP).

Legislation

There is no major legislation so far intended for Internet content. The Dutch believe that most of the Internet crimes in the Netherlands can be covered by existing laws. Nevertheless, there have been intergovernmental activities. For example, the ministries of Education, Culture and Science, together with those of Public Health, Welfare and Sports, are preparing a paper outlining policies in dealing with the protection of minors in audiovisual media. At the same time, the ministries of Justice and of Transport, Public Works and Water Management are also collaborating with Parliament to develop guidelines to prevent the distribution of illicit material on the Internet.

Self-Regulation

Dutch self-regulatory efforts are based on an idea of mass public awareness and active participation. Among the initiatives taken are hot lines set up by NLIP, CRI and NBRD. The general public is then encouraged to call in and report any objectionable materials. The hot-line staffers, originally volunteers but now professionals, check the reports received against the consortium's guidelines and criteria. If the report made meets the stated criteria, a series of graded steps can be taken, starting with a warning sent to the person or persons posting the objectionable material, requesting they remove the material within one week. If no action is taken by the responsible party, then a second tier of policy actions may be taken, which may include the filing of a complaint to the local police for action.

In dealing with materials originating from outside the Netherlands, hot-line staffers again contact the author of the material; in addition they notify the ISP who registered the author. If no action is taken by the author in a specific time frame, the hot-line staffers may notify the Dutch police, who notify their police counterpart in the concerned foreign country to take up the matter.

Use of Rating System

The Dutch Association of Internet Providers (DAIP) is studying the labeling and filtering systems with a view toward recommending the systems to the public. Meanwhile individuals can buy such systems if they need them.

Belgium

In contrast to the Netherlands, Belgium has been active both on the legislative and self-regulatory fronts.

Legislation

Two actions have been or are in the process of being taken by the Belgium legislature. One involves the revision of the Belgium Penal Code to combat child pornography through information services. The second is a draft bill now under consideration by the Belgium Parliament, again revising information technology. The bill will put down a legal framework to fight criminal activities in information technology, including on the Internet. The Belgium government also believes in international cooperation and has encouraged discussions and initiatives at the European Union and OECD levels.

Following existing laws, Belgium police run a hot line where the public can report objectionable material in all media, including the Internet, and the police follow up on these reports.

Self-Regulation

The self-regulatory efforts in Belgium are led by the Internet Services Providers Association of Belgium (ISPA), a body formed by the Belgium ISPs. ISPA intervenes between the general public and the law enforcement agencies, the police in this case. ISPA works with the police and the ministers of justice and Telecom on one hand and the public on the other.

Singapore

Although Singapore entered the global Internet arena late in 1994 with the introduction of the Singapore Telecom's Singnet service, the Internet has been embraced by the government in its IT2000 project, aimed at making Singapore an information society in the shortest time possible. This strong government involvement in Internet activities has brought the strong arm of government regulatory measures onto the Internet and has perhaps received unproportional global attention over the last couple of years mainly because most people outside Singapore see these measures as censorship of the Internet. Unlike other countries we have seen so far, whose main objectives are to prohibit illicit and illegal material on the Internet, in particular child pornography and hate speeches, the Singapore intentions are a bit broader. Singapore justifies stringent measures on the basis that the Internet as a broadcast medium, as a communication medium and a computer services medium has tremendous potential for stirring up and starting problems for the people of Singapore. They fear that, like any mass broadcast medium, the Internet could be used to stir up religious, cultural and political unrest (13).

Legislation/Licensing

In 1996 the government of Singapore started a class-licensing system under which Internet services providers (ISPs), just like any other mass broadcast medium, must register with the Singapore Broadcasting Authority (SBA), which was given sole authority to oversee the system. As a result of this directive, the SBA has issued Internet content guidelines called *Class License Scheme*, which every ISP must adhere to. The scheme was deemed an automatic licensing scheme, whereby services would automatically be deemed licensed and ISPs must comply with the license conditions. The Class License Scheme was meant to encourage responsible use of the Internet while facilitating its healthy development. It encourages minimum standards in cyberspace and seeks to protect users, especially the young. The scheme puts ISPs into three categories:

1. Internet Access Service Providers (IASPs): to include all providers licensed under the Telecommunication Authority of Singapore
2. Localized Internet Service Providers (LISPs): to include all those who provide Internet services to the general public in specific public places like libraries

3. Non-localized Internet Service Providers (NISPs): to include all mid-providers who get services from the IASPs and resell them to subscribers

In addition to the ISP categories, there are also the Internet Content Providers (ICPs), who provide information on the World Wide Web. All ISP categories are required to be licensed, whereas content providers are not. Under the scheme all ISPs must provide information and accept an understanding required by the SBA. Such an undertaking includes the ISPs' commitment to use their best efforts to ensure that (a) the services they provide comply with the code of practice issued by the SBA, and (b) their servers are not used for any purpose or program that is against public interest, public order or national harmony, and those that offend the public. This system is being applied to non–Singaporean services outside Singapore as long as such services target Singapore citizens. For a full text of the Class License Scheme and guidelines see http://www.gov.sg/sba.

Self-Regulation

One can say that the SBA is a self-regulatory body, but given the close relationship between it and the government, perhaps the SBA is working more as an enforcer of the state machinery than as a self-regulating body. However, the SBA encourages the use of filtering software.

China

China entered the Internet arena late, in 1993, and its Internet experience, adventure and plans are a mixture of amazement and concern. Since 1989 the Chinese telecommunication infrastructure has been growing at an annual rate of 30 percent to 50 percent, adding an average of 10 million telephone connections annually (14). In addition to this impressive growth, China has embarked on an ambitious national infrastructure initiative, code-named the "Gordon Projects," to build its own Internet. However, before it realizes its own Internet, China is trying to control access and content of the current global Internet, of which it is a member.

According to Zixiang Tan et al. (14), Chinese Internet policy is driven by the desire to "balance gradual commercialization and modernization with controls protecting the Communist Party ideological dominance." This policy is based on a paradox: Under a banner of "economic informatization," Chinese leaders have come to realize and accept that information technology should be a driving force towards future Chinese economic development. At the same time, they understand that informatization comes with a price — the risk and potential for the central government's losing control of the flow of information. To implement this policy China has chosen a two-pronged approach: regulation through a series of measures, and blocking.

Legislation/Licensing

China's legislative efforts are anchored by two state council class orders and directives from the state premier. Between them they form three regulatory regimes:

1. State Council Order No. 147 of 1994: Security Regulations for Computer Information Systems in the People's Republic of China. This order, meant to strengthen national security, directs the ministry of public security (MPS) to require every individual who wants to set up an Internet account or simply use the Internet in an Internet Cafe, to file a police report within thirty days of the establishment of a link, which is then sent to the local MPS and then the provincial MPS Computer Security Supervision Office (14). Reporting changes and terminations of linkages is also required (15). The order further requires new Internet users to sign a Net Access Responsibility Agreement, swearing not to threaten the security of the state, reveal secrets or do anything that endangers public safety or is obscene or pornographic. It also requires all users with dial-up Internet accounts to provide their ISP permit for the modem they are using (14).

2. State Council Order No. 194 of 1996: Interim Regulation on International Interconnections of Computer Information Networks in the Peoples' Republic of China. This order assigned all issues concerning computer communication in the People's Republic of China to the State Council's Leading Group of Economic Informatization. This leading group was charged, among other things, with the coordination and decision making on international interconnection issues, including defining rights, obligations and liabilities of international interconnection channel providers, interconnecting organizations, accessing organizations and users (14). To achieve this the order divided all the country's computer networks into two categories: interconnecting networks (INs), those networks linked to the Internet through leased circuits, and access networks (ANs), the Internet ser-

vice providers (ISPs). Under directive 195 all INs are to be controlled and administered by one of four organizations: Ministry of Posts and Telecommunications (MPT), the Ministry of Electronic Industries (MEI), the State Education Commission (SEC) and the Chinese Academy of Sciences (CAS). As a result of directive 195, China's INs are now spread around four organizations: SEC's China Education and Research Network (CERNET), MPT's ChinaNET, CAS's China Science and Technology Net (CSTNET) and MEI's China Golden Bridge NET (ChinaGBN). Each of the INs has a focused agenda; both ChinaNET and ChinaGBN focus on commercial interests, and CSTNET and CERNET focus on academic and scientific interests (14, 16). Unlike the INs, which can make direct connections to the International Internet, the ANs must get their connections via the International In-and-Out Administration, the nation's major supervising office comprising the INs forming the National Public Telecommunications Network (17). Each member in the Public Communication Network issues relevant regulations vented by the State Council Leading Group to the INs they are connecting (18).

3. In May 1997 Premier Li Peng imposed regulations requiring all those doing business on the Internet in China to apply for licenses (14).

Blocking/Filtering

Besides directives and decrees, China also blocks Internet content. Ironically, the blocking and filtering efforts have local ISP and IS professional support (14). Chinese blocking techniques follow a two-tier approach: the government requiring Internet browsers for distribution in China to include blocking tools, and government using their own blockers (19). Also recently China blocked about 100 Internet sites (20).

Australia

In 1995 a Senate Select Committee of the government of the Commonwealth of Australia on Community Standards Relevant to the Supply of Services Utilizing Electronic Technologies deliberated and came up with a comprehensive policy, in the form of recommendations, for the government of the Commonwealth and those of the states and territories in dealing with electronic technology.* Although the recommendations of this committee are mostly self-regulatory because they considered the Internet as an online service and not as a broadcasting service, they stress the need for legislative measures to complement the codes of practice developed by industry and used in self-regulatory systems. Here are the recommendations of that committee (21):

Recommendation 1: that the Commonwealth, State and Territories legislate to make it an offense to use a computer service to transmit, obtain possession of, demonstrate, advertise or request the transmission of material which is or is likely to be Refused Classification (RC) or to be in a restricted category it is likely to cause offense to a "reasonable adult" as described in the National Classification Code.

Recommendation 2: that an independent complaints handling body be established under the purview of the ABA or other appropriate government body, based on the model provided by the Telephone Information Services Standards Council (TISSC), to deal with complaints from users of computer on-line services.

Recommendation 3: that the Minister for Communications and the Arts introduce legislation, modeled on the Broadcasting Services Act of 1992 to require participants in the on-line industry to develop codes of practice which address certain basic principles to be formulated in consultation with participants in the on-line industry, to abide by them and to require those codes of practice to be registered with an appropriate body to be determined in the legislation.

Recommendation 4: that the legislation governing the registration of codes of practice should include provisions for financial penalties (of up to $100,000) to be imposed for breaches of those codes of practice.

Recommendation 5: that the legislation should contain provisions designed to protect from prosecution, those Internet Service Providers who choose, in good faith, to restrict access to material that while not illegal, could cause offense.

Recommendation 6: that legislation developed as per recommendation 3 above should make it mandatory for those who make available restricted material through on-line services to require a pin

---

Recommendations of the Senate Select Committee on Community Standards Relevant to the Supply of Services Utilizing Electronic Technologies, Parliament of the Commonwealth of Australia, chaired by Senator John Tierney. Source: http://www.senate.aph.gov.au/committee/comstand/online/recom.htm

number (which will be available only on production of a driving
license or other proof of age) before granting the user access to such
material.

Recommendation 7: that the Minister for Communications and the
Arts direct the ABA to investigate the development of reliable age
verification procedures for accessing material not suitable for children
through on-line services.

Recommendation 8: that all States and Territories amend their
Classification and/or Censorship legislation to make it an offense to
transmit objectionable material and to cover the transmission of
material unsuitable for minors through computer on-line services so
that all States and Territories would have legislation that is uniform
according to an agreement to be reached by the On-Line Government
Council, and adopt a standard definition of the expression: "objectionable material."

Recommendation 9: that, once all States and Territories have enacted
legislation as per recommendation 8 above, designated units in State
and Territory police forces should conduct random audits of material
on-line for illegal activities.

Recommendation 10: that the On-Line Ministerial Council agree
to commit the Commonwealth and States to funding an on-line advertising campaign to accompany the implementation of any regulatory
measures adopted by the Council and the Standing Committee of
Attorney-Generals. The campaign must provide information for
Internet users to make them aware of existing legislation and their
legal obligations.

Recommendation 11: that federal legislation requiring the development of codes of practice for the on-line industry (as per recommendation 3) should also require retailers and service providers to provide
information to customers on blocking and filtering devices and any
other method that are or become available to manage children's access
and block out material they may not wish to access.

Recommendation 12: that any community education campaign that
is conducted to encourage the responsible use of on-line services should
have as one of its aims to make parents and those responsible for children aware of the pros and cons of the various devices available on the
market for blocking access to material considered by some to be unsuitable.

Recommendation 13: that the Minister for Communications and the Arts request (under Section 171 of the Broadcasting Services Act 1992) that the Australian Broadcasting Authority convene an On-Line labeling Task Force (to include representatives of the Office of Film and Literature Classification (OFLC) and representatives of the on-line services industry) to design a scheme for labeling on-line content that takes into account Australian cultural values and the principles that govern the existing classification scheme.

Recommendation 14: that the ABA or another appropriate government body establish an e-mail, phone and fax hot line service to receive information about possible illegal material (including pedophilic material and child pornography) found by users on the Internet.

Recommendation 15: that the Australian government continue its discussions in international fora with the aim of developing an international Agreement aimed at facilitating co-operation between countries in developing protocols for pursuing criminal activities carried out through the use of computer on-line services.

Legislation

The Australian federal government has not as yet acted on any legislation concerning online services. There is a belief that existing laws are adequate, although some legislations are likely to come out of the recommendation of the Senate Select Committee on Community Standards Relevant to the Supply of Services Utilizing Electronic Technologies. For example section 85ZE of the Commonwealth Crimes Act of 1914 says that no person shall knowingly or recklessly (a) use a telecommunication service supplied by a carrier to menace or harass another or (b) use a telecommunication service supplied by a carrier in such a way as would be regarded by reasonable persons as being in all circumstances offensive (21).

Although at the federal level there are no specific legislations to regulate online services, at the state and territory level there is an active program for legislations. For example, the states of Victoria and Western Australia and the Northern Territory have enacted legislations that cover transmission of materials on online services. These legislations make it an offense to (a) transmit objectionable materials, (b) transmit to minors materials unsuitable to minors, or (c) advertise that objectionable material is available for transmission (21).

In particular, Western Australia and the Northern Territory define an offense in this category as any one of the following:

1. transmission of articles knowing that they are objectionable material
2. being in possession of articles with the knowledge that they are objectionable material
3. demonstrating an article with the knowledge that it is objectionable material
4. advertising objectionable materials
5. requesting the transmission of materials knowing that they are objectionable materials
6. using a computer service to make available and to transmit restricted materials to minors

In Victoria an offense in this category is any one of the following:

1. use of online services to publish, transmit or make available objectionable materials, including advertisements and notices
2. knowingly allowing an online service to be used for publishing, transmitting or making available for transmission advertisements or notices of objectionable materials
3. use of online services to publish, transmit or make available objectionable materials to minors

Self-Regulation

Following the 1995 recommendation of the Senate Select Committee on Computer Regulation of Online Services for the Development of a System of Self-Regulation for the Online Industry, a flurry of self-regulatory activities started in Australia. For example, the Australian Broadcasting Authority (ABA) in its 1996 recommendation to the minister of communication and the arts strongly recommended a system of self regulation based on codes of practice by industry and also that such codes be registered by the Authority. A number of online industry players responded to this recommendation, including the Internet Industry Association of Australia (INTIAA) and the Committee of Australian University Directors of Information Technology (CAUDIT).

INTIAA is positioning itself to be the prime leader in IT-industry, leading awareness campaigns and lobbying for the industry at state and federal levels. The INTIAA code found at http://www.iniaa.asn.au/codeV2.htm is very comprehensive and addresses a wide variety of complex issues in the industry. It is based on classification and labeling in accordance with the National Classification Code (NCC). It requires each member of the INTIAA, called Code Subscriber, to operate within the NCC, ensuring that labeled materials or would-be labeled materials are

1. segregated and have clearly identifiable signatures that can be recognized by network management filters,
2. accompanied by suitable onscreen warnings on a Web page, which appear to the user before the content can be viewed,
3. managed by subscription enrollment to exclude under-age subscriptions.

And further guarding minors, ISPs must

1. not knowingly provide unrestricted access to the Internet to users under the age of 18 years without the written permission of parents or guardians,
2. request for age verification for over 18 years and access to the Internet will be supervised by persons over 18 years old,
3. take reasonable steps to verify the age of each user by requiring every new user at signon to confirm the age requirement. (21)

The code, if adopted in its present form, will make the ISPs responsible for classification of online materials in accordance with the National Classification Council (NCC) and also give them the authority to give or deny access to the unclassifiable or rejected classification (RC) materials. Of course with self-regulation arises a need for compliant handling; the Senate Select Committee recommended a model like the Telephone Information Service Council (TISSC) to handle complaints and settle disputes.

Canada

Legislation

Canada has yet to pass a single law specifically targeting the Internet, although there is a debate on the proposed privacy legislation. There is widespread belief that different services provided by the Internet and technology, including suppliers, can be covered by one or more of the existing policies and laws. Industry Canada, in a paper entitled "The Cyberspace Is Not a 'No Law Land,'" has published a comprehensive review of all Canadian laws applicable to the Internet. The emphasis has therefore been on self-regulation. However, Canada, like its neighbor to the south, is deeply embroiled in a debate about Internet content and the nature of the Internet. For Canada, which prides itself on its cultural heritage, the debate revolves around the "convergence" of the media brought about by the Internet. According to the Canadian Association of Internet Providers, the concept of convergence implies an increasing overlap between the two components of the communications systems; the common carrier system and networks referred to as the "conduit"- and "content"-based information services and technologies.

For a long time in Canada, "conduit" and "content" have been treated differently, the former as telephony and the later as broadcasting. The telecommunication, that is the "conduit," component is regulated through the *Telecommunications Act* in order to achieve economic objectives by forbidding carriers to interfere with "content" in transition. However, to protect Canadian identity and culture, broadcasting is regulated via the *Broadcasting Act*, requiring broadcasters to be heavily involved in "content." Naturally the debate revolves around "conduit" and "content" in the converged media of the Internet. The issues are mainly the definition of the Internet content — whether such content is "programs" and therefore covered by the *Broadcasting Act* or not and, hence, under the jurisdiction of the *Telecommunications Act*.

Self-Regulation

The Canadian Association of Internet Providers (CAIP) is the main engine behind self-regulatory measures in Canada. CAIP preempted government legislation when it developed a code of conduct and promised that its members will voluntarily commit themselves to (a) cooperate with the efforts of government, international organizations and law enforcement agencies and (b) comply with all existing applicable laws that cover the activities on the Internet. See the code at http://www.caip.ca/caipcode.htm.

United States

U.S. Internet policy can be viewed through two rather confusing, intricate and incompatible delivery structures. The first is the hierarchical few-to-many communication infrastructures on which historically all major communication media like telecommunication, television and radio broadcasting and newspapers are based. This structure has been in place for generations, and the social, cultural, political and economic fabrics of the United States are built on it. The second is the newer and flat many-to-many communication infrastructure based on newly developed computer and digital communications technologies. It has no history, no track record, no central authority, no management and no control, and it is most exemplified by the Internet. As we have seen throughout this book, the Internet structure is a "functioning anarchy" that has yet to follow an established norm of communication, management and control. Besides lacking central authority, management and control, this delivery infrastructure consists of three delivery media: telecommunication, broadcasting and computer services.

Evolving Internet policy, therefore, seeks to reflect and incorporate the attributes of each structure because each offers some economic, social, political and cultural advantages. Noting that the first structure currently anchors American social, cultural and political systems, and realizing that the second structure, that is the Internet, has exhibited more democratic potential than the first ever did, and given the democratic ideals of the United States, together with the difficulties associated with attributes of these structures, it is highly unlikely that the new policy will closely follow either one of the two. However, based on the unlimited potential of the Internet and the speed of technological changes, it is more likely that the new policy may carry more of the Internet's attributes than those of the first structure.

In the formulation of the new policy, so far, there seem to be a bit of both in that after the court defeat of the Communication Decency Act (CDA), Internet regulatory pressures were eased a little to focus more on self-regulatory mechanisms, where Internet service providers (ISPs) and individual users are the principal players just like in the first structure, where telecommunication, television, radio and newspaper executives were in charge of regulating the content transmitted.

However, although the policy trends seem to be heading towards self-regulation, this does not mean there have not been and continue to be regulatory efforts to control Internet content. Battles are being fought between two equally vocal and determined groups: the free-speech advocates, who favor a free, unregulated Internet, and the anti-pornography group. Although evolving Internet policy is not directly based on the agendas of these groups, concerns from both groups will be reflected in the new policy agenda, as will the commercial interests that have so far been given an unfair advantage. From what has been coming in the news, it looks like all sectors of the federal government are emphasizing that the

Internet, as a communication, broadcast and computer services media will be built, owned and operated by the private sector. The strongest indication yet of this policy came from the working paper on Internet policy by Kevin Werbach, Federal Communications Commission consul for New Technology, entitled "Digital Tornado: The Internet and Telecommunications Policy" (22). "Digital Tornado" was a serial FCC paper designed to help frame debate on the Internet policy in a procompetitive context. The central theme of the paper is that because the Internet "is not tied to traditional models or regulatory environments, it holds potential to drastically change the communication landscape. The Internet creates new forms of competition, valuable services for the end users, and benefits to the economy. Government policy approaches toward the Internet should, therefore, start from two premises: avoid unnecessary legislation and question the applicability of the traditional rules" (22).

Indeed, in the wake of the CDA defeat in courts, the Clinton administration has been shifting policy from its previous support for using the federal government to restrict access to indecent materials on the Internet to a more self-regulated Internet (23). In fact, this was the philosophy that led to the National Science Foundation's (NSF) ceasing its support of the Internet. This thinking has also been strengthened by high-ranking government and U.S. Congress officials. For example, Newt Gingrich, Speaker of the U.S. House of Representatives, in support of a free-enterprise-driven Internet, argues that "profits are synonymous to public service," and Al Gore, U.S. vice president, also argues "that there are public interest concerns the marketplace cannot resolve but can only be addressed after the profitability of the dominant corporate sector has been assured" (24).

Keeping in mind that perhaps the views of these two public officials represent the views of the two dominant political parties in the United States, one wonders what the views of the average citizens are. A glimpse of their thinking can be inferred from an unscientific survey conducted on *CNN Interactive*, an online service of CNN, in the wake of the defeat of the CDA. The results of the survey showed strong indications that the public considered CDA unconstitutional and did not favor it. They did not consider Internet pornography a serious enough problem to warrant control of the Internet by government, and they believed that the overall responsibility of control of the Internet is with the parents or seniors, like teachers (25). If this survey is any indication of the feeling of the U.S. public, the message is consistent with views already articulated by Kevin Werbach of the FCC. Let us survey what has been happening so far.

Legislation

At the federal level U.S. legislative efforts are highlighted by the highly charged, debated and now defeated Communication Decency Act (CDA) bill below.

This Communications Decency Act of 1996 is a section of the Telecommunications Act of 1996, passed by Congress on January 31 as Senate Bill S.652 as sent to the President.*

Telecommunications Act of 1996

TITLE V — OBSCENITY AND VIOLENCE

Subtitle A — Obscene, Harassing, and Wrongful Utilization of Telecommunications Facilities

SEC. 501. SHORT TITLE.

This title may be cited as the "Communications Decency Act of 1996."

SEC. 502. OBSCENE OR HARASSING USE OF TELECOMMUNICATIONS FACILITIES UNDER THE COMMUNICATIONS ACT OF 1934.

Section 223 (47 U.S.C. 223) is amended —

(1) by striking subsection (a) and inserting in lieu thereof:

"(a) Whoever —

"(1) In interstate or foreign communications —

"(A) by means of a telecommunications device knowingly —

"(i) makes, creates, or solicits, and

"(ii) initiates the transmission of, any comment, request, suggestion, proposal, image, or other communication which is obscene, lewd, lascivious, filthy, or indecent, with intent to annoy, abuse, threaten, or harass another person;

"(B) by means of a telecommunications device knowingly —

"(i) makes, creates, or solicits, and

"(ii) initiates the transmission of, any comment, request, suggestion, proposal, image, or other communication which is obscene or indecent, knowing that the recipient of the communication is under 18 years of age, regardless of whether the maker of such communication placed the call or initiated the communication;

"(C) makes a telephone call or utilizes a telecommunications device, whether or not conversation or communication ensues, without disclosing

Source: Library of Congress: http://thomas.loc.gov/cgi-bin/query/z?c104:s.652.enr:

his identity and with intent to annoy, abuse, threaten, or harass any person at the called number or who receives the communications;

"(D) makes or causes the telephone of another repeatedly or continuously to ring, with intent to harass any person at the called number; or

"(E) makes repeated telephone calls or repeatedly initiates communication with a telecommunications device, during which conversation or communication ensues, solely to harass any person at the called number or who receives the communication; or

"(2) knowingly permits any telecommunications facility under his control to be used for any activity prohibited by paragraph (1) with the intent that it be used for such activity, shall be fined under title 18, United States Code, or imprisoned not more than two years, or both; and

"(2) by adding at the end the following new subsections:

"(d) Whoever —

"(1) in interstate or foreign communications knowingly —

"(A) uses an interactive computer service to send to a specific person or persons under 18 years of age, or

"(B) uses any interactive computer service to display in a manner available to a person under 18 years of age, any comment, request, suggestion, proposal, image, or other communication that, in context, depicts or describes, in terms patently offensive as measured by contemporary community standards, sexual or excretory activities or organs, regardless of whether the user of such service placed the call or initiated the communication; or

"(2) knowingly permits any telecommunications facility under such person's control to be used for an activity prohibited by paragraph (1) with the intent that it be used for such activity, shall be fined under title 18, United States Code, or imprisoned not more than two years, or both.

"(e) In addition to any other defenses available by law:

"(1) No person shall be held to have violated subsection (a) or (d) solely for providing access or connection to or from a facility, system, or network not under that person's control, including transmission, downloading, intermediate storage, access software, or other related capabilities that are incidental to providing such access or connection that does not include the creation of the content of the communication.

"(2) The defenses provided by paragraph (1) of this subsection shall not be applicable to a person who is a conspirator with an entity actively involved in the creation or knowing distribution of communications that violate this section, or who knowingly advertises the availability of such communications.

"(3) The defenses provided in paragraph (1) of this subsection shall not be applicable to a person who provides access or connection to a facility, system, or network engaged in the violation of this section that is owned or controlled by such person.

"(4) No employer shall be held liable under this section for the actions of an employee or agent unless the employee's or agent's conduct is within the scope of his or her employment or agency and the employer (A) having knowledge of such conduct, authorizes or ratifies such conduct, or (B) recklessly disregards such conduct.

"(5) It is a defense to a prosecution under subsection (a)(1)(B) or (d), or under subsection (a)(2) with respect to the use of a facility for an activity under subsection (a)(1)(B) that a person —

"(A) has taken, in good faith, reasonable, effective, and appropriate actions under the circumstances to restrict or prevent access by minors to a communication specified in such subsections, which may involve any appropriate measures to restrict minors from such communications, including any method which is feasible under available technology; or

"(B) has restricted access to such communication by requiring use of a verified credit card, debit account, adult access code, or adult personal identification number.

"(6) The Commission may describe measures which are reasonable, effective, and appropriate to restrict access to prohibited communications under subsection (d). Nothing in this section authorizes the Commission to enforce, or is intended to provide the Commission with the authority to approve, sanction, or permit, the use of such measures. The Commission shall have no enforcement authority over the failure to utilize such measures. The Commission shall not endorse specific products relating to such measures. The use of such measures shall be admitted as evidence of good faith efforts for purposes of paragraph (5) in any action arising under subsection (d). Nothing in this section shall be construed to treat interactive computer services as common carriers or telecommunications carriers.

"(f)(1) No cause of action may be brought in any court or administrative agency against any person on account of any activity that is not in violation of any law punishable by criminal or civil penalty, and that the person has taken in good faith to implement a defense authorized under this section or otherwise to restrict or prevent the transmission of, or access to, a communication specified in this section.

"(2) No State or local government may impose any liability for commercial activities or actions by commercial entities, nonprofit libraries, or institutions of higher education in connection with an activity or action described in subsection (a)(2) or (d) that is inconsistent with the treatment of those activities or actions under this section: Provided, however, that nothing herein shall preclude any State or local government from enacting and enforcing complementary oversight, liability, and regulatory systems, procedures, and requirements, so long as such systems, procedures, and requirements govern only intrastate services and do not result in the imposition of inconsistent rights, duties or obligations on the provision of interstate services. Nothing in this subsection shall preclude any State or local government from governing conduct not covered by this section.

"(g) Nothing in subsection (a), (d), (e), or (f) or in the defenses to prosecution under subsection (a) or (d) shall be construed to affect or limit the application or enforcement of any other Federal law.

"(h) For purposes of this section —

"(1) The use of the term "telecommunications device" in this section —

"(A) shall not impose new obligations on broadcasting station licensees and cable operators covered by obscenity and indecency provisions elsewhere in this Act; and

"(B) does not include an interactive computer service.

"(2) The term 'interactive computer service' has the meaning provided in section 230(e)(2).

"(3) The term 'access software' means software (including client or server software) or enabling tools that do not create or provide the content of the communication but that allow a user to do any one or more of the following:

"(A) filter, screen, allow, or disallow content;

"(B) pick, choose, analyze, or digest content; or

"(C) transmit, receive, display, forward, cache, search, subset, organize, reorganize, or translate content.

"(4) The term 'institution of higher education' has the meaning provided in section 1201 of the Higher Education Act of 1965 (20 U.S.C. 1141).

"(5) The term 'library' means a library eligible for participation in State-based plans for funds under title III of the Library Services and Construction Act (20 U.S.C. 355e et seq.)."

SEC. 507. CLARIFICATION OF CURRENT LAWS REGARDING COMMUNICATION OF OBSCENE MATERIALS THROUGH THE USE OF COMPUTERS.

(a) IMPORTATION OR TRANSPORTATION — Section 1462 of title 18, United States Code, is amended —

(1) in the first undesignated paragraph, by inserting "or interactive computer service (as defined in section 230(e)(2) of the Communications Act of 1934)" after "carrier"; and

(2) in the second undesignated paragraph —

(A) by inserting "or receives," after "takes";

(B) by inserting "or interactive computer service (as defined in section 230(e)(2) of the Communications Act of 1934)" after "common carrier"; and by inserting "or importation" after "carriage."

(b) TRANSPORTATION FOR PURPOSES OF SALE OR DISTRIBU-
TION — The first undesignated paragraph of section 1465 of title 18,
United States Code, is amended —

(1) by striking "transports in" and inserting "transports or travels in, or
uses a facility or means of,";

(2) by inserting "or an interactive computer service (as defined in section
230(e)(2) of the Communications Act of 1934) in or affecting such commerce" after "foreign commerce" the first place it appears;

(3) by striking "or knowingly travels in" and all that follows through
"obscene material in interstate or foreign commerce," and inserting "of."

(c) INTERPRETATION — The amendments made by this section are
clarifying and shall not be interpreted to limit or repeal any prohibition
contained in sections 1462 and 1465 of title 18, United States Code, before
such amendment, under the rule established in United States v. Alders,
338 U.S. 680 (1950).

SEC. 509. ONLINE FAMILY EMPOWERMENT.

Title II of the Communications Act of 1934 (47 U.S.C. 201 et seq.) is
amended by adding at the end the following new section:

"SEC. 230. PROTECTION FOR PRIVATE BLOCKING AND
SCREENING OF OFFENSIVE MATERIAL.

"(a) FINDINGS — The Congress finds the following:

"(1) The rapidly developing array of Internet and other interactive computer services available to individual Americans represent an extraordinary
advance in the availability of educational and informational resources to
our citizens.

"(2) These services offer users a great degree of control over the information that they receive, as well as the potential for even greater control in
the future as technology develops.

"(3) The Internet and other interactive computer services offer a forum for
a true diversity of political discourse, unique opportunities for cultural
development, and myriad avenues for intellectual activity.

"(4) The Internet and other interactive computer services have flourished,
to the benefit of all Americans, with a minimum of government regulation.

"(5) Increasingly Americans are relying on interactive media for a variety
of political, educational, cultural, and entertainment services.

"(b) POLICY — It is the policy of the United States —

"(1) to promote the continued development of the Internet and other
interactive computer services and other interactive media;

"(2) to preserve the vibrant and competitive free market that presently exists for the Internet and other interactive computer services, unfettered by Federal or State regulation;

"(3) to encourage the development of technologies which maximize user control over what information is received by individuals, families, and schools who use the Internet and other interactive computer services;

"(4) to remove disincentives for the development and utilization of blocking and filtering technologies that empower parents to restrict their children's access to objectionable or inappropriate online material; and

"(5) to ensure vigorous enforcement of Federal criminal laws to deter and punish trafficking in obscenity, stalking, and harassment by means of computer.

"(c) PROTECTION FOR 'GOOD SAMARITAN' BLOCKING AND SCREENING OF OFFENSIVE MATERIAL —

"(1) TREATMENT OF PUBLISHER OR SPEAKER — No provider or user of an interactive computer service shall be treated as the publisher or speaker of any information provided by another information content provider.

"(2) CIVIL LIABILITY — No provider or user of an interactive computer service shall be held liable on account of—

"(A) any action voluntarily taken in good faith to restrict access to or availability of material that the provider or user considers to be obscene, lewd, lascivious, filthy, excessively violent, harassing, or otherwise objectionable, whether or not such material is constitutionally protected; or

"(B) any action taken to enable or make available to information content providers or others the technical means to restrict access to material described in paragraph (1).

"(d) EFFECT ON OTHER LAWS —

"(1) NO EFFECT ON CRIMINAL LAW — Nothing in this section shall be construed to impair the enforcement of section 223 of this Act, chapter 71 (relating to obscenity) or 110 (relating to sexual exploitation of children) of title 18, United States Code, or any other Federal criminal statute.

"(2) NO EFFECT ON INTELLECTUAL PROPERTY LAW — Nothing in this section shall be construed to limit or expand any law pertaining to intellectual property.

"(3) STATE LAW — Nothing in this section shall be construed to prevent any State from enforcing any State law that is consistent with this section. No cause of action may be brought and no liability may be imposed under any State or local law that is inconsistent with this section.

"(4) NO EFFECT ON COMMUNICATIONS PRIVACY LAW — Nothing in this section shall be construed to limit the application of the Electronic Communications Privacy Act of 1986 or any of the amendments made by such Act, or any similar State law.

"(e) DEFINITIONS — As used in this section:

"(1) INTERNET — The term "Internet" means the international computer network of both Federal and non–Federal interoperable packet switched data networks.

"(2) INTERACTIVE COMPUTER SERVICE — The term "interactive computer service" means any information service, system, or access software provider that provides or enables computer access by multiple users to a computer server, including specifically a service or system that provides access to the Internet and such systems operated or services offered by libraries or educational institutions.

"(3) INFORMATION CONTENT PROVIDER — The term "information content provider" means any person or entity that is responsible, in whole or in part, for the creation or development of information provided through the Internet or any other interactive computer service.

"(4) ACCESS SOFTWARE PROVIDER — The term "access software provider" means a provider of software (including client or server software), or enabling tools that do any one or more of the following:

"(A) filter, screen, allow, or disallow content;

"(B) pick, choose, analyze, or digest content; or

"(C) transmit, receive, display, forward, cache, search, subset, organize, reorganize, or translate content."

This CDA bill, which was approved by the U.S. Congress and quickly signed into law a few days later by President Clinton, was intended to bar indecent materials from the Internet by punishing those who distribute to minors obscene or indecent materials over the Internet with a fine of $250,000 and a two-year prison sentence. The bill was immediately challenged in federal court by a number of free-speech advocate groups, which include the American Civil Liberties Union (ACLU), the Electronic Frontier Foundation (EFF), the American Library Association (ALA), EPIC and many others on grounds that the bill placed an unconstitutional ban on free speech.

The three federal judges sided with the plaintiffs and temporarily blocked the enforcement of the law, saying that the Internet is already covered by the First Amendment. Following the first court decision against CDA, battle lines were drawn between those who supported free speech — contending that the Internet should be classified as a print media for which there are already laws on books, including the First Amendment — and the antipornography camp, supported by the government, who contended that the courts should treat the Internet as a broadcast medium because of its use of telecommunications lines on which Internet images flow, and therefore more restrictions should be applied to it, since images are more accessible to children. The action of the lower federal court was later upheld by the U.S. Supreme Court, which decisively struck down CDA to the joy of free-speech advocates. However, the legislative fights are not over. The states are already actively pursuing their own legislations. Besides the states, Congress may even try again to rewrite a new CDA, taking into account those objections by the Supreme Court in the now defunct CDA.

Self-regulation

The defeat of the CDA in courts gave a new impetus to the self-regulatory drive. Immediately after the court decision, the White House came up with a new Internet draft policy that stated, "Because filtering devices are available to let parents limit what their children can view, it is not necessary to extend content restriction similar to radio or television to the Internet" (26). To further make the point, the White House — together with talent and expertise from a wide variety of who's who in corporate America and civic groups, including America Online, Microsoft, Disney, AT&T, the American Library Association, the National Education Association, Children Now, the Urban League and others — convened the Internet/Online Summit to enhance the safety and benefits of cyberspace for children and families. Two initiatives undertaken by the summit were to enhance law enforcement and to educate the public on Internet safety. Both these initiatives are self-regulatory. The summit saw the role of ISPs, in making the Internet a safe place for children, taking center stage. The online industry, mostly ISPs, agreed to play their role by policing the Internet and reporting activities involving child pornography to law enforcement agents. Under the policy adopted at the summit, ISPs would remove child pornography from their bulletin boards and services (27). Besides the White House other government agencies have followed the same line of thought. The Federal Trade Commission (FTC) agreed not to impose regulations governing the Internet, citing the ever-changing technology. Similarly other government bodies, including the Federal Communications Commission (FCC), the Federal Reserve Board (FRB) and the Securities and Exchange Commission (SEC), have also decided to self-impose standards in a few cases (28).

Private initiatives are also in high gear. In the corporate arena both Microsoft and Netscape Communications, the two largest Internet browser powerhouses, have pledged to adhere to PICS standards by embedding support for PICS in all their future releases of Internet browsers. The National Association of Securities Dealers (NASDAQ) has formulated its own Internet law to cover every security dealer.

Blocking/Filtering

The United States leads the world in the development of Internet blockers and filters. This, together with the fact that close to 60 percent of all Internet activities are in the United States, supports a conclusion that the rate of blocking and filtering on an individual basis is high. The use of filters was further boosted by the Internet/Online Summit.

Hot Lines

One of the fruits of the Internet/Online Summit was the formal establishment of a hot line at the National Center for Missing and Exploited Children. This 800 number (1-800-843-5678) is toll free. Besides the telephone number, the National Center Web site also reports incidents of child sexual exploitation, including pornography.

Kenya

Although Internet activities in most African countries are just starting and are still limited to a small elite class most often unnoticed by governments, there are some indications of Internet controls in some countries. This should not come as a surprise because most African countries have a track record of media controls, Kenya being among such countries.

Legislation

Kenya has a vibrant Internet, and Internet activities are beginning to catch the attention of the government, which has begun to put controls on the Internet similar to those in other media, like newspapers, radio and television. To this end, according to Mike Jensen, the Kenyan Communications Commission has imposed a stiff fee on all ISPs, requiring them to pay about one half million Kenyan shillings for the license in addition to 1 percent of their gross turnover for an operating fee. ISPs are also required to provide the commission with a list of their clients' names and addresses (29).

Chapter 6

A Look into the Future

The Future of the Internet

Predicting the future of the Internet, from what we know of it so far, is like looking in a crystal ball and predicting the future of any living person. The prediction remains uncertain. However, unlike the individual's future predictions, which may cause anxiety, the Internet's future causes excitement because those who have embraced the Internet think that it is likely to bring greater and more positive, uplifting applications to humanity.

There is a widely held belief, mostly in the United States, that the future of the Internet as a new data highway will improve the competitiveness of the U.S. manufacturing base, speed the efficiency and security of electronic commerce and inter- and intrabusiness communications, improve health delivery systems, help to contain skyrocketing medical costs, foster and promote better educational systems both in delivery and administration and help in efficient delivery of government services. These are but a few of the beliefs of many governments and individuals around the globe. Although these beliefs may vary, they summarize the great expectations of the human race about the Internet. To glimpse the future of the Internet, let us look at what it may look like in the following areas:

Access and Growth

Currently there are close to 600 million telephone connections globally, and this number is growing as more communities gain better technology (1). Industry experts predict that all these telephone lines will eventually be connected to the Internet, wiring a significantly larger portion of the world population than the current 30–40 million connections. Some of these telephone connections will be in public places and kiosks available to mass access. This is already happening in countries like Holland. This concept of mass access will open the Internet to yet a larger population. Anticipating this growth, and backed by experience and success of current Internet technology, a group of U.S. universities, together with the U.S. government and industry, have joined together to form a partnership that aims to develop the next Internet technology, termed Internet2, based on the Next Generation Internet (NGI) Initiative developed by the Large Scale Networking Working Group of the Computing Information and Communication R&D Subcommittee. According to the concept paper of this committee (see http://www.ccic.gov/ngi/concept-Jul97/), Internet2 will connect at least 100 NGI sites — universities, federal research institutions, and other research partners — at speeds 100 times faster than today's Internet. In accepting the initiative, the U.S. government was reacting to the belief that the current Internet suffers from its own success, using over-stretched networks designed to serve thousands but now serving millions. Many scientists and engineers believe that new technologies, protocols and standards can be developed for the next generation Internet to offer reliable, affordable and secure information delivery at rates thousands of times faster than today. To reach that vision, there are three goals for this NGI initiative, each with a strategic approach and each with metrics of success (2):

1. Experimental Research for Advanced Network Technologies: To promote experimentation with the next generation of network technologies through development and demonstration of advanced network service technologies needed to support next-generation applications.

2. Next Generation Network Fabric: To develop a next-generation network test bed to connect universities and federal research institutions at rates sufficient to demonstrate new technologies and support future research.

3. Revolutionary Applications: To demonstrate a wide variety of nationally important applications that cannot be achieved over today's Inter-

net. Ideally these applications will include federal agency mission applications, university and other public sector applications and private sector applications.

When fully operational the project will have developed a new family of advanced applications to meet new requirements in research, teaching and learning by

1. creating and sustaining leadership in network capacity for research without competing with commercial interests as the case is on the current Internet,
2. directing network development efforts to come up with a new generation of real-time, interactive applications that can work well with and exploit broadband network media integration,
3. integrating the capabilities and work of Internet2 with those of the current Internet to be able to transfer those applications to all levels of educational use to a global Internet community,
4. creating advanced network services to meet the requirements of broadband, networked applications for industry through campus-based and regional universities' collaboration (3).

When fully operational, Internet2 is expected to be a thousand times faster than the current Internet, using advanced fiber-optic cables connected to super-high-speed points known as GigaPOPs like the conceptual model shown in Figure 6.1 on the following page.*

Business and Commerce

After the National Science Foundation ceased support of the current Internet and the networks were privatized commercial interests in the Internet skyrocketed. This exponential growth of commercialization of the Internet has led many to predict that the future of the Internet is in business and commerce. A study by Information, Communication and Entertainment suggests that the Internet will stimulate a high level of electronic commerce (4). In addition to the growth of Internet commerce, activities between businesses will also grow tremendously through instant access to essential business information on products, services, prices and customers. Besides electronic commerce and inter- and intrabusiness communication, the Internet's future also promises to involve and expand service businesses.

Internet2 Service Center is used by permission of Information Resources and Communications, University of California.

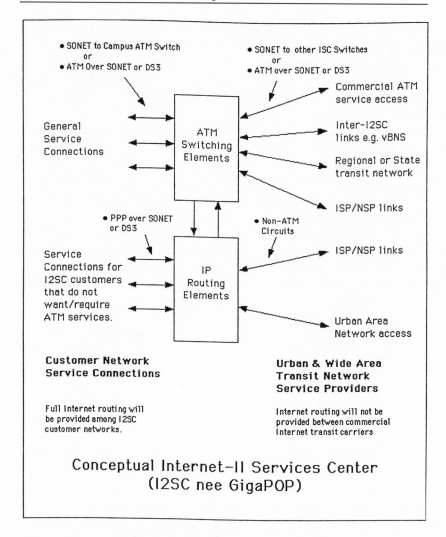

Figure 6.1 Internet2 Service Center

Service companies, most notably online companies, are working to make the Internet as easy to use, as accessible and as critical to personal and business communications as the telephone company did a couple of years ago. By doing this these service companies are slowly pulling individuals and businesses into the Internet web, thus making us chronically dependent on the Internet.

Knowledge

With the predicted expansion and better, easier and cheaper access, the pool of knowledge available on the Internet is expected to expand tremendously.

However, the media through which knowledge has been stored and transmitted and a number of other knowledge attributes will undergo remarkable changes in order to meet the expanding Internet. Some of these changes may include the following:

1. Print Medium

    The demise of the print medium is already in progress with the onslaught of digital information. For example, the volume of e-mails on the Internet now rivals the U.S. Postal System, and e-mail growth is unprecedented. So the era of the book and the centuries-old image of a library seem to be on their way out.

2. Quality and Quantity

    Traditionally there has been a limited supply of knowledge on just about anything, and it has been difficult to get information on just about anything. So the general wisdom has been "You want it? You pay for it" because information entrepreneurs involved in collection, compilation and storage of knowledge invested a lot of time and money in their enterprises. With Internet technology, information collection, compilation, processing and storage have undergone a revolution, making the acquisition of knowledge easy and cheap. Besides the ease and declining costs of acquiring knowledge, quantity of knowledge has increased tremendously. This quantity, however, has been a double-edged sword because on one hand, the abundance of information creates awareness and makes information and subsequent knowledge acquisition cheap, but on the other hand, it creates an imbalance between the quantity of available information and the amount of information that the human mind can absorb at any one time. This runaway information avalanche, or "infoglut," has surpassed the technology of the networks to process it fast enough due to limitation in bandwidth. The future of the Internet will see action in this direction by creating new tools to select, refine and store only needed information.

3. Consequential Illiteracy

    Historically we have defined illiteracy as not being able to read or write any language, a Gutenberg print-era malady. Computer technology and indeed the Internet are redefining this concept. In colleges we now call it computer illiteracy or computer dysfunctionality and phrases like these. We are evolving a new definition of consequential illiteracy, a new definition for illiteracy in the digital Internet age. As truckloads of knowledge are dumped on our doorsteps every day via the Internet, keeping current is extremely difficult, both physically and financially, due to ever-evolving new access methods and machinery. Even so, staying illiterate is likely to be more expensive than staying literate in today's medium.

Our Role in the Future Internet

Luciano Floridi has conceptualized the Internet as a new country with a growing population of millions of well-educated citizens with no need of highway patrol or central authority (5). So in order for this country to keep its cultural, social, political and civic achievements and see them grow in the new environment, every citizen must demonstrate a high degree of involvement in the efficient management of the country. Such management could and must involve a knowledge management system that prioritizes individual responsibility and autonomy. These goals could be acquired through the shared efforts of all citizens of this global community, through what is being currently done and beyond, as we have seen throughout this book. These concerns of the future and the need for consolidated efforts are supported by the results of a study done by the Information, Communication, and Entertainment (ICE(sm)), which showed that security and privacy concerns undermined the confidence created by the rosy projections of the goods the future Internet will deliver to humanity (4,5). In the study transaction security was the leading concern, followed by information privacy. As I have pointed out throughout the book, the current trend to control the Internet is still voluntary and basically self-regulatory except in a few countries, but this may change with time, better technology and probably unseen events and circumstances.

1. Legislation Efforts Will Continue

The current failure of efforts to legislatively regulate the Internet, brought about by the depleting court defeats of the U.S.'s Communications Decency Act (CDA) and France's Telco Act or the Fillon's Amendment, does not mean that the battle between the free-speech advocates and the antipornography groups is over. Already in the

United States there is Sen. Dan Coats's bill, which will require all commercial Web sites carrying materials judged harmful to minors to block their access or face criminal penalties. Such a bill automatically makes the ISPs the Internet police. Other members of the U.S. Congress are about to try to fashion a new version of the CDA, termed *CDAII,* that would more likely withstand the court objections found in the defeated bill, and similar efforts are probably taking place in France and elsewhere.

2. Boost Self-Regulation

On a different track, self-regulation supporters are likely to be boosted by the new brand of both software and hardware applications that will enhance the capabilities of blocking and filtering indecent and objectionable materials on the Internet. There are already signs pointing to this strategy. In the United States, for example, after the defeat of the CDA, the White House changed its policy from legislative to self-regulatory control, citing the increasing availability of filtering and blocking devices and software to boost parental control of Internet content (6). The recent White House–supported Internet/Online Summit boosted the Internet's self-regulatory efforts. The summit's two initiatives, to enhance law enforcement and to educate the public on Internet safety, were a shift away from the strong legislative tactics the administration had previously embarked on when it supported the Communications Decency Act.

3. Mass Education Targeted

Beyond the battlefields of free-speech and antipornography groups, other efforts not directly involving solid control, nonregulation, and free-access schemes should continue. These efforts include the concerted efforts in both formal and informal planned education and mass-education campaigns by advocacy groups and the use of hot lines.

4. In the Long Run

Martin Bangemann, commissioner for the European Union, has proposed an international statute based on self-imposed regulations by businesses and states and a common set of general rules. The proposed general rules in the charter would deal with issues on technical standards, illegal content, licenses, encryption and data privacy on the Internet and other electronic carriers and networks. This statute, if adopted, represents a patchwork of business, national, civic and individual rules, guidelines, cannons and codes embracing different cultures, religions and languages. No one knows whether such a mosaic of rules will ever work in unison. One thing is clear, though: the best solution to the Internet wars is likely to be home-grown and self policed.

Notes

1. The Structure and Development of the Internet

1. Barry M. Leiner, Vinton G. Cerf, David D. Clark, Robert E. Kahn, Leonard Kleinrock, David C. Lynch, Jon Postel, Larry G. Roberts, Stephen Wolff. *A Brief History of the Internet.*
Http://www.isoc.org/internet-history/
2. Bruce Sterling. *A Brief History of the Internet.*
Http://www.viv.com/Demo/SterlingBrief.htm
3. Cheung Harvey Wai-Lun. *X.25 Packet Transmission Protocol.*
Http://bugs.wpi.edu:8080/EE535/
4. *About the InterNIC.*
Http://rs.interNIC.net/interNIC/index.html.

2. Internet Globalization and Its Effects on Societies

1. Larry Press. "Tracking the Global Diffusion of the Internet." *Communications of the ACM* 40, no. 11 (1997): 11–17.
2. Robert Fox. Newstrack — "Top-10 Languages in Cyberspace." *Communications of the ACM* 40, no. 11 (1997): 10.

3. Micheal Peirce. "Payment Mechanisms Designed for the Internet." Http://ganges.cs.tcd.ie/mpeirce/Project/oninternet.html

4. AfricaLink. "New Communication Technology Project Helps Save Lives in Africa." Http://www.info.usaid.gov/alnk/

5. Eran B. Scenker. "Virtual Reality and Telemedicine in What Stage Are We?" Http://www.med.wright.edu/som/resident/asm/iamirr.html.

6. Stephen Ndegwa Mwangi. "Cyber University Launched." *Computers in Africa*, November 1997.

3. The Internet as a Global Medium: Concerns

1. Richard Rubin, "Moral Distancing and the Issue of Information Technologies: The Seven Temptations," in Joseph M. Kizza, *Social and Ethical Effects of the Computer Revolution* (Jefferson, N.C.: McFarland, 1996), 124–135.

2. "U.S. Said Vulnerable to Computer Attack," *CNN-Interactive*, October 21, 1997. Http.//cnn.com/TECH/9710/21/cyberwars.ap/index.html

3. Ian Davis. "Crime and the Net." Http://www.law.ttu.edu/cyberspace/jour10.htm

4. Marty Rimm. "Marketing Pornography on the Information Superhighway." Http://TRFN.pgh.pa.us/guest/mrtxt.html

5. Phillips Elmer-Dewitt. "Cover Story: On a Screen Near You: Cyber Porno." Http://pathfinder.com/

6. "Software Piracy," Business and the Network, *Investor's Business Daily*, June 23, 1997. Http://www.ibm.com/OtherVoices/Investors_BN/June23973817.html

7. John Levine. "Why Spam Is Bad." Http://www.spam.abuse.net/spam/spambad.html

8. "AOL Wins Injunction Against Spammer," *CNN-Interactive*, Nov. 4, 1997 (See also http://cnn.com/744).

9. CNN (Sci-Tech). "Internet Fraud." Http://cnn.com/Tech.9706/09/Internet/

10. "Internet Code Deemed Vulnerable to Hackers," *CNN-Features.*

11. "Virtual Gaming Patterns: The Gaming Industry."
Http://cnn.com/TECH/
(See also http://www.createandconsult.com/gaming1.html).

12. "Cyberspace Attacks Threaten National Security, CIA Chief Says," *CNN-Interactive*, June 25, 1996.
Also at http://cnn.com/Tech/9606/25/comp.security/index.html

13. Rory J. O'Connar and Knight Ridder. "Report Says U.S. Open to Computer Threats," Wednesday, October 22, 1997.
Http://www.virtuallynw.com/stories/1997/Oct/22/S296177.asp

14. Kenneth C. Laudon. "Privacy," *Communications of the ACM* (Sept. 1996): 72.

15. Abraham Edel, Elizabeth Flower and Finbarr W. O'Connar. *Morality, Philosophy and Practice: Historical and Contemporary Readings and Studies* (New York: Random House, 1989).

16. *Time.* Jan 18, 1993.

17. Rusty Dormin. "Debate Rages Over Electronic Access to Public Records."
Http://cnn.com/Tech/9608/17/public.privacy/index.html

18. Joseph M. Kizza. *Ethical and Social Issues in the Information Age* (New York: Springer, 1997).

19. Bruce Schneir. "Cryptography, Security and the Future," *Communications of the ACM,* 40.6 (1997): 138.

20. Hal Berghel. "Cyberspace 2000," *Communications of the ACM.* 40.2 (1997): 19–24.

21. Kathy Nellis. "Expert Information Onslaught Bad for Your Health," *CNN-Interactive*, April 15, 1997.
Also at http://cnn.com/Tech9704/information.overload/

4. The Internet as Global Media: Regulation and Control Tools

1. New Dimensions International. "U.S. Lacks Tools vs. Computer Attack." Reuter.
Http://www.infowar.com/CIVIL_DE/civil_062097a.html-ssi

2. "Cyberspace Attacks Threaten National Security, CIA Chief Says," *CNN-Interactive*, June 25, 1996.
Also at http://cnn.com/Tech/9606/25/comp.security/index.html

3. "40 Million Potential Spies: Internet Opens Gates to Pentagon Computers," *CNN-Interactive*, June 23, 1996.

Also at http://cnn.com/TECH/9606/23/internet.spying/index.html

4. William H. Murray. "View Point: Who Holds the Key?" *Communications of the ACM* 35, no. 7 (1992): 13–15.

5. Paul Fahn. "Answers to FAQ About Today's Cryptography." Http://www.rsa.com/pub/faq/faq.asc/

6. National Institute of Standards and Technology. "The Digital Signature Standards: Proposed by NIST," *Communications of the ACM* 37, no. 7 (1992): 36–40.

7. Philip R. Zimmerman. *The Official Guide to PGP*. MIT Press, 1995.

8. "Administration, Computer Industry Pledge Anti-Smut Efforts." *CNN-Interactive*, July 16, 1997.

9. "A New Babble Over Keeping the Web Clean." Http://cnn.com/TECH/9708/07/Internet.decency.lat/index.html

10. RSAC. "Four Easy Steps in the RSACi Rating Process." Http://www.rsac.org/fra_content.asp?onIndex=8

11. Micro System Software, Inc. "CyberPatrol CyberNOT list Criteria." Http://www.handiware.com/cyber/cp-list.htm

5. Regulating the Internet: National and Regional Efforts

1. "Resolution Adopted by the Telecommunication Council, February 1997." Http://www2.echo.lu/legal/en/internet/content/resol.html

2. "Final Report of the Information Highway Advisory Council," Information Highway, Canada. Http://strategis.ic.gc.ca/ssg/ih01070e.html

3. "Government and Industry Back Internet Watchdog," Internet Watch Foundation, Press Release, July 28, 1997.

Also at http://www.internetwatch.org.uk/press.html

4. R³-Safety-Net. "Illegal Material on the Internet." Http://www.ispa.org.uk/safetypa.html

5. Internet Watch Foundation. "Introduction." Http://www.internetwatch.org.uk/intro.html

6. "French 'Conseil Constitutionnel' Decision: Unconstitutionality of Fillon's Amendment."

Http://www.aui.fr/English/Press/constit-25-july.html

7. AUI Press Release, May 8, 1996.

Http://www.aui.fr/English/press.usenet-8may.html

8. Lionel Jospin. "Preparing France's Entry into the Information Society."

Http://www.tagish.co.uk/ethos/news/lit1/9782.htm

9. "The French Charter."

Http://www.tagish.co.uk/ethos/news/lit1/9f3a.htm

10. "Silencing the Net." Human Rights Watch 8, no. 2(G) (May 1996). Also at http://www.netfreedom.org.ua/anoid/stneuro.htm#france

11. Michael Schneider. "Internet Content Task Force (ICTF)," Press release, September 3, 1996.

Http://www.anwalt.de/ictf/p960901e.htm

12. Michael Schneider. "Background Behind Internet Media Council and Internet Task Force (ICTF)."

Http://www.anwalt.de/ictf/e-introl.htm

13. Peng Hwa Ang and Berlinda Nadarajan. "Censorship and the Internet: A Singapore Perspective." *Communications of the ACM* 39, no. 6 (1996): 72–78.

14. Zixiang Tan, Milton Mueller, and Will Foster. "China's New Internet Regulations: Two Steps Forwards One Step Back." *Communications of the ACM* 40, no. 12 (1997): 11–16.

15. "Supervision of the Internet Stepped Up." *INET-L Newsletter*, no. 62, March 3, 1996.

Http://www.cnd.org:8012/CND-China/CND-China.96-03-03.html

16. "China Issues New Rules to Regulate Links to Internet." *INET-L Newsletter*, no. 61, February 16, 1996.

Http://www.cnd.org:8012/CND-China/CND-China.96-02-16.html

17. "Management of China's Internet Strengthened." *INET-L Newsletter*, no. 70, July 2, 1996.

Http://www.cnd.org:8012/CND-China/CND-China.96-07-02.html

18. "Ministry Formulating Regulations for Information Networking." *INET-L Newsletter*, no. 72, August 2, 1996.

Http://www.cnd.org:8012/CND-China/CND-China.96-08-02.html

19. "US Companies Meet Dilemma as China Regulates Internet Access." *INET-L Newsletter*, no. 74, October 20, 1996.

Http://www.cnd.org:8012/CND-China/CND-China.96-10-20.html

20. "Internet Censorship Likely to Fail." *INET-L Newsletter*, no. 74, October 20, 1996.

Http://www.cnd.org:8012/CND-China/CND-China.96-10-20.html

21. "Report on Regulation of Computer Online Services, Part 3." Senate Select Committee on Community Standards Relevant to the Supply of Services Utilizing Electronic Technologies. Parliament of the Commonwealth of Australia, June 1997.

Http://www.senate.aph.gov.au/committee/comstand/online/index.htm

22. Kevin Werbach. "Digital Tornado: The Internet and Telecommunications Policy," FCC Staff Working Paper on the Internet Policy, March 27, 1997.

Http://www.fcc.gov

23. "White House Readies New Policy for Internet Decency." *CNN-Interactive*, June 16, 1997.

Also http://cnn.com/TECH/9706/16/comm.decency.act/

24. Robert McCheney.

25. "Communications Decency Act Opinion Poll," *CNN-Interactive*.

Http://cnn.com/US/9703/cda.scotus/poll.verdict/index.html

26. "What's Next in Washington: More Legislation Likely But Clinton May Withdraw Support." *CNN-Interactive*, March, 1997.

Http://cnn.com/Us/9703/cda.scotus/beyond.cda/what.next.html

27. Jeri Claising. "Gore Announces Efforts to Patrol Internet," *Pointcast Network*, December 3, 1997.

Http://127.0.0.1:15841/

28. Mike Yomamoto. "After CDA Ruling, Net Polices Itself," *The Net*, June 15, 1997.

Http://www.news.com/SpecialFeatures/0,5,1574,00.html

29. Mike Jensen. "Internet Africa: Kenya KCC Fees Hit ISPs." *Computers in Africa*, May, 1997.

30. Private Communication from Diane Whitehouse.

6. A Look into the Future

1. "Special Report: The Future of the Internet." *Freedom Magazine*, 27(4). Church of Scientology International.

Also at http://www.freedommag.org/english/vol2704/future.htm

2. "Next Generation Internet Initiative," NGI Concept Paper, July 23, 1997.

Http://www.ccic.gov/ngi/concept-Jul97/

3. Internet2: Project Description.

Http://www.Internet2.edu/html/project-description.html

4. "Internet's Future Looks a Lot Like Business."

Hhttp://www.drive-outline.com/netfut.htm

5. Luciano Floridi. "The Internet and Future of Organized Knowledge: Part 3 of 3."

Http://www.valdosta.peachnet.edu/~wihuitt/psy702/files/Internet3.html

6. "Administration, Computer Industry Pledge Anti-Smut Efforts." *CNN-Interactive*, July 16, 1997.

Also at http://cnn.com/Tech/9707/16/anti.smut/index.html

7. Reuters. "U.S. May Back Internet Charter, Not Formal Body," Reuters, October 2. Also *The Netly News* at

http://cgi.pathfinder.com/netly/latest/RB/1997Oct02/250.html

Index

AEH 2707